CRY *for* RAIN

a memoir

The true story of soul-consuming,
bitter, childhood battles within
a young girl's home amidst
Iran's political and religious upheavals

Melineh Petrosian

Dear Lynette,

Thank you for your support.

Melineh Petrosian

2018

ELECTIO PUBLISHING
first century principles.
a twenty-first century approach.

D1224177

Cry for Rain

By Melineh Petrosian

Copyright 2018 by Melineh Petrosian. All rights reserved.

Cover Design by eLectio Publishing. Photo by Lane Erickson. Used by permission.

ISBN-13: 978-1-63213-492-9

Published by eLectio Publishing, LLC

Little Elm, Texas

http://www.eLectioPublishing.com

5 4 3 2 1 eLP 22 21 20 19 18

The eLectio Publishing creative team is comprised of: Kaitlyn Hallmark, Emily Certain, Lori Draft, Court Dudek, Jim Eccles, Sheldon James, and Christine LePorte.

Publisher's Note

The publisher does not have any control over and does not assume any responsibility for author or third-party websites or their content.

In memory
of my loving nephew, Ivan

Put your head on my shoulder,
Let me wipe your tears.
Tuck your forehead to my chest,
Let my heart bleed for you.

Let me hold your hands to comfort you.
And when your cross is heavy,
Let me carry it for you.

You've got your wings,
Fly away.
I never knew how large a space you occupied,
It can never be filled.

Miss you.

For Papa, who will never read this book.

Also, for my sister, Eda, and her ongoing support and love.

And for my brothers, Ed and Josh, with whom I share many painful childhood memories.

Acknowledgments

A special thanks goes to my gracious husband and amazing children for their love and support. To my critique group, Fern Brady, Landy Reed, Frank Chambers, Ollie Stevenson, Araceli Casas, Raul Herrera, Verstandt Shelton, Beabe Thompson, and Connie Gillen, for their powerful input. To my agent, Jeanie Loiacono, who took her time to read my story, give it a voice, and believe in me. To Christopher Dixon and Jesse Greever of eLectio Publishing, whose backing transformed my story into a book. And most of all, to an extraordinary woman, Aimee Malek, who believed in me and stood by me every step of the way, who encouraged me, read with me, and edited for me. Without you, this would not be possible.

And I thank my Lord, for He has blessed me.

Prologue

RAIN POUNDS AT MY WINDOW from a grayish-green sky. The leaves of the palm trees bend down, bowing to the wild wind's demands. Violent thunder shakes the window as spears of lightning illuminate the storm-darkened garden beyond.

As I sit on the couch, wrapped in my soft brown blanket, a cup of coffee in my hand, I open a box filled with old photographs. Sifting through the stack, I come across some pictures of me as a little girl, when we used to live in our old house. My sister, my brothers, Papa, Mom, and my only friend, Hamlet, appear in many of them.

At a very young age, my siblings and I learned that to survive, we had to be obedient and protect one another. These photos are reminiscent of the bitter days of Mom's heartless punishments; days filled with fear from her unpredictable anger. Most of all, they are a reminder of my stolen childhood and unfortunate teenage years.

Sadness engulfs me. Quiet tears roll down my face. I catch them with the sides of my fingers before they drop on the pictures. I look to see if there are any forgotten photos. That's when I find some from my middle-school years. One picture shows my friends and me singing the national anthem. We look solemn, but I smile, recalling how we were really admiring the king and queen's royal crowns. Another depicts my sister, after joining the Shah's army, dressed in her khaki uniform and lavender bandana. I grab another picture. This one's from high school. I am there along with the new students who had lost their homes due to the war with Iraq.

Despite the tyranny of Iran's regime, we never anticipated any other ruler. Remembering the radical change to an Islamic government under Khomeini's rule, I am amazed. Gone were dreams of the future. Focusing on daily living became our goal. We were trying to adjust to changing from a westernized kingdom to a religious, anti-western government. As if that was not enough, Iran's seemingly eternal conflict with its neighbor meant we also had to cope with Iraqi fighter jets' continual bombing.

My life had its own battlefield. Besides the new Islamic government and a war-torn country, Mom's abuse, narcissism, and psychotic behavior at home left me no safe place to shelter.

The sound of thunder draws my attention to the backyard. I see my reflection in the window and I remember all the pain, the loss, the numbered joys. As I take a sip from my coffee, my eyes fall upon a small picture of Hamlet sitting on the floor near the Christmas tree, running his choo-choo train.

At that moment, the urge to write rushes through my veins, so I begin. I write so I can share my journey of disappointments from which I found a thread of hope.

1968–1969
Home

I WAS BORN IN 1963, in the Islamic capital of Iran, Tehran. Our family was part of the Christian minority. My parents, sister, brother, and I lived in a rental house owned by a Christian landlord, in the northern part of the city, close to the mountains. The winters were cold with heavy snow and icy roads, spring was full of life, summers were cool, and autumn's foliage was a myriad of color.

I am now four years old.

The rental house was located by the river, with a narrowly paved walkway leading to an old wooden door with blue paint that had been aged by the sun and rain. A metal ring hung from the door. When handled, it would dangle and bounce, announcing a visitor. Past the door was a courtyard with a little pond surrounded by flowerbeds. In a far nook stood a quince tree. During autumn and winter, it was adorned with golden, apple-like fruit covered by a thin layer of fuzz that released a unique aroma. There also grew a lilac bush and an evergreen.

On the north side of the courtyard stood our landlord, Arman's, newly built house. He and his wife, Miss Mary, had a little boy with brown eyes and short, dark hair, named Hamlet, who was my age. He was my *only* playmate. He had his own bedroom with a big bed and a dark blue, handmade quilt with matching pillows, a desk, and lots of toys. On good days, he let me play with them. The one toy I'd do anything to play with was his choo-choo train. Just getting to turn on the train and watch it move around the rails made me so happy! On his bedroom wall hung a beautiful picture of Jesus Christ with a crown of thorns and blood dripping down his forehead. That picture always mesmerized me. And it's in that room where Miss Mary taught me how to pray. Besides his room and toys, I loved their bathroom. I'd go there and wash my hands just because they had hot water. My little hands wouldn't freeze like they did in my house.

On the other side of the courtyard, my house had one bedroom, which belonged to my mom and papa, and one formal dining room with doors that remained permanently closed. We could go there only if Mom let us, which only happened on special occasions. Most of our time was spent in the living area where we ate, studied, and slept. Its furniture included a wooden table, six chairs with blue seat cushions, and a small, dark cabinet with serving dishes inside. Our bedding consisted of woolen mats, a duvet, and feather pillows. When not in use, they were folded and neatly kept behind a curtain in the corner of the room.

Our small kitchen was nothing like Hamlet's. Over there, I always felt safe and happy. It was a cozy place where Miss Mary let us have cake or ice cream while she was cooking. My kitchen was always cold and dark. Devoid of love, it was just another one of Mom's domains from which she ridiculed and cursed her children.

We did not have a shower. Instead, we had a small area behind the kitchen with a small, yellow water tank, which had to be filled manually, and a sink. That's where my mom would give us a bath. In this so-called "bathroom," there was a small window facing the sidewalk, but we could never see outside since it sat too high on the wall. I loved that window! Anytime someone passed by, we could hear their footsteps. This meant we could always hear my papa coming home. Funny how we never mistook his footsteps for another's. We'd run to the entry door, and as soon as my papa got close, we'd open it and greet him. Actually, I would jump into his arms and he would toss me in the air and lift me onto his shoulders before we'd walk inside. Oh, how I loved those moments. But Mom never did. I remember one such homecoming . . .

As if provoked, Mom angrily orders Papa, "Put that spoiled brat down!"

Still smiling, Papa ignores her command. Even though I feared Mom's rage, the joy of standing on my papa's shoulders is all mine to keep.

We enter the living room that way, where Papa gently puts me down on the floor. I keep hold of his big strong hand real tight, rubbing my little face against it, knowing what is coming. It happens almost every time.

Mom stomps in after us and snatches my long ponytail, dragging me away from Papa, saying, "How many times have I told you not to get on his shoulders, you brat?"

"Why are you doing this, Liz? What has she done? Let her go."

Papa always sounds calm as he tries to release my hair from her hold. My sister, Eda, intervenes, taking my hand, and we go off to hide in the corner of the living room. She wraps her arms around me, comforting and protecting me. On the other side of the room, my brother, Ed, stands frozen in fear, his small, dark eyes brimming with tears. I hide my face in Eda's body but peek to see what is about to happen.

Mom screams at Papa, "I hate you! And I hate your kids! My life is miserable, and you caused it! I hope you die, and your kids, too! I hope I bury you all!"

She gazes at us, clenching her teeth. The look on her face scares me. We all know she is furious. That's when she opens the small cabinet door, pulls out glasses and plates, and begins to smash them into the wall and floor. Some of them break; others are just damaged. The shattering noises scare me, and I cover my ears. Mom's black hair, once pulled back tightly in a bun, now hangs messily around her face and her hands tremble.

Papa tries to calm her down by asking, "What is wrong with you? That's enough. What is the matter? What do you want?" He shakes his palms to the ceiling.

Mom starts crying hysterically. "I'm tired of these animals!" she yells, pointing at us. "You're always gone! Never around! Even when you are home, all your attention is for the kids. It's never about me!"

Papa is quiet now. My brother, sister, and I wait for this storm to pass. Eda and I look at each other. Her beautiful brown eyes are red and swollen, and her thin body trembles, but she still holds me tight. With her gentle fingers, she wipes away my tears. In her arms, I feel safe. I don't want her to let go. I turn my face to see what Ed is doing. He still is standing in the corner, and I see the worried look on his face. He steals glances at us, longing to come closer but afraid to move, as it might draw her attention.

The silence makes us think it's over. Ed takes a step toward us. Mom jumps at him and grabs his ear and slaps him across the face.

With a firm voice, Papa says, "Liz, that's enough."

Mom shrieks, "See? This is why my life is miserable! This damn boy cannot stay still for a second!" She slaps Ed again, and he cries out in pain.

Papa steps in, separating Ed from Mom. Ed runs to us. Mom continues wailing as Papa holds her hands and leads her to sit down on a chair. He gestures with a quick hand behind his back for us to leave the room. Inching along the wall, the three of us make our way to the balcony door.

It's almost dark outside. We sit at the edge of the balcony. Ed and Eda dangle their feet, and I sit hugging my knees to my chest. None of us speaks. Ed holds his red, bleeding ear where Mom pinched it with her fingernails.

Eda whispers, "Go wash your face and hands."

"I'm okay," Ed says, trying hard not to cry.

"You're getting blood all over."

"But if I move, Mom might see me."

Eda lets go of my hand and leans toward Ed. Grabbing his hand, she forces him to stand, and they go down the stairs to the backyard faucet and she helps him wash up.

I walk quietly toward the living room door, trembling with fear. I get up on my tiptoes, wanting to see Papa. I can hear him talking to Mom.

"Liz, please. This is my job. I have to go on trips to make money for you and the kids. Driving a truck is all I know." His voice is so calm. "Do you think for one minute how uncomfortable my life is out there? I sleep on the seat of my truck. I can't even stretch my legs. If the weather and mosquitoes permit, I can sleep stretched out on the truck's flatbed. Of course, when I do that, I have to worry about thieves. Please pull yourself together," Papa begs, his hand held out palm up.

I am still behind the door. Ed and Eda slowly come toward me as the door opens, then Papa is in front of us.

"Come on in, children. Come on in. Your mother is fine." He stands back so we can enter.

I turn around, looking at Ed and Eda, debating whether or not we should go inside. Papa taps my arm and I follow him in with Ed and Eda behind me.

Mom is quiet now. Papa calmed her down . . . this time. Ed, Eda, and I are relieved. I hope Papa won't leave us tomorrow because I know that as soon as he does, Mom will start on another of her rampages. All three of us dread the day when he has to go on his next job.

Broken Smiles

DAYS WITHOUT PAPA, Ed, and Eda are so long and boring. I'm too little to go to school, so Eda gives me homework before she and Ed leave each day, something simple like tracing the alphabet letters. This keeps me busy for a while, until Mom starts giving me chores. Sometimes it's sweeping the kitchen floor or separating the peas from their pods. Other times, I break the pasta into thirds, so that Mom can cook it. Every once in awhile, she takes me to the grocery store. But when Mom is done with me, I am expected to sit quietly near her. It's so hard for me to sit still. I don't even know if Mom remembers that I am here.

Today, as soon as Ed and Eda leave for school, Mom tells me, "Ariana, help me clean the breakfast dishes and tidy up the house, so we can go to the bazaar. I have some shopping to do."

"Are you buying me new shoes?" I ask.

"No, I'm not. I will get you some for Easter. Now hurry up and help me fold these sheets and blankets."

Soon, the house is clean and organized. I'm so anxious to go shopping.

"Here. Change into this shirt and your pink, pleated skirt."

I start dressing myself as Mom changes her housedress to a brown dress with orange-flowered trim and a beige cardigan. She makes all of her own dresses and ours, too. She then brushes her dark hair and pulls it back into a headband.

"Come here, Ariana. Sit on the floor, and I'll help you put on your tights."

She then fixes my hair into a tight ponytail, and we're ready to go.

We walk to the alley and on to the street. It's windy and chilly, so Mom wraps my coat around me.

"Mom, what are you going to buy?"

"Some underwear and socks for all of you." She raises her hand in the air and hails, "Taxi! Taxi!"

A yellow car stops in front of us.

"Hurry up, Ariana! Get in!"

I climb into the back seat next to an old man, then Mom slides in next to me. I keep watching the man play with a string of beads between his fingers, reminding me of my grandma's prayer beads.

After a while, in Farsi, Mom asks the driver to stop. She pays him and we climb out.

"Ariana, stay close to me, and don't wander around. Bad people may snatch you away."

"Oh no, Mom. I'll stay close to you." I don't really know what she means, but I hold her hand tightly.

We pass through the noisy crowd from store to store. There are so many people shopping and motorists riding their motorcycles, weaving in and out between people and shouting words I don't know. Since we always speak Armenian at home, I don't understand much of the Farsi everyone else speaks.

"Come closer, Ariana. I need to buy something in this store."

Holding Mom's hand, I follow her inside. She stops and begins going through a pile of socks on a table. Many people pass by when suddenly, a tall woman comes and stands very close to us. She wears a black chador that covers her from head to toe. Before I know it, she grabs my hand and pulls me away from Mom, hiding me under her black cover.

"Come on. Good girl," the woman says in Farsi.

"No! No! Mom!" I cry. I can't see anything except for the asphalt below me.

"Stop your crying," she orders, and keeps pulling my hand.

"Mom! Mom!" I scream louder.

The woman stops for a second, opens her cover, and now I can see the crowd. She points in the distance.

"Look, see that big, green gate? When we get there, I will buy you an orange soda."

I like that drink, and I can almost taste it, but I still want my mom.

She covers me again underneath her chador and moves forward. After a while, I hear a man's voice shouting, "Stop that woman! She stole away a little girl! Stop her!"

I cry harder. Then I hear my name. "Ariana! Ariana!" I recognize my mom's voice, and I scream at the top of my lungs. The woman covers my mouth with her hand. Suddenly, we stop, and I am pulled out from under her cover.

Mom runs over to me, wraps me in her arms, and holds me tight. She then turns to the bad woman and spits at her. "Shame on you! How could you do this to a little girl?" she scorns, as the woman in black flees.

"God bless you, sir," Mom says to the man who rescued me. "Thank you. What would I have done without your help?"

***

As soon as Ed and Eda arrive home from school, Mom says to them, "Today, Ariana and I went to the bazaar, and a terrible woman snatched her! I was going crazy, and I almost passed out."

In a worried voice, Eda says, "Really, Mom? How did you find her?"

"When I noticed she wasn't beside me, I screamed and started calling for her. People gathered around me, and one man spoke out, saying that he had seen her. He began running after the woman. Thank God, for that man."

"Mom, was she going to sell Ariana to bad people behind the green gate?" Ed asks.

"Of course. That's what they do," Mom replies.

Eda comes closer and wraps her arms around me. "Thank God you are safe," she whispers in my ear. We all sit together and share our snack of little cheese sandwiches and tea. It's not long before they must do their homework.

Eda pauses to ask Mom, "What is the big green gate for anyway?"

Mom replies, "Beyond that gate, child molesters and prostitutes live. Law forbids them to interact with society, so they are separated from us all." I don't really understand any of what they are talking about, but it makes me feel uneasy.

The three of us sit at the table that is only used for doing homework or accommodating the occasional guests who might come over for dinner or tea. As we take our seats, Mom comes and settles between Ed and Eda. I'm at the end of the table with four colored pencils and an old notebook. This time, I try to trace the numbers that Eda has made for me.

I love this because when I am done, and if it is pretty, Eda will give me a shiny star sticker. She saves up her allowance that Papa gives her and buys them just for me. Mom really doesn't care that much. And from time to time, she takes away Eda's money to punish her for spending it stupidly.

Eda sits with her head down. Her shoulder-length, silky, brown hair covers her face, but I can see her pretty, sculpted nose. She has one hand on her book and writes with the other. Ed works on his math problems. Mom crochets, glancing at their work from time to time.

"What is that you wrote?" Mom asks Eda.

Eda stops writing and looks at Mom, glancing confusedly at her notebook, unclear as to what Mom is asking.

Mom turns to Eda and backhands her in the mouth. "I am asking you, animal, what are you writing? Answer me!"

Eda covers her mouth and whispers in a shaky voice, "I wrote 'Taj Mahal.'" Tears and blood drip onto her paper.

Mom shouts, "Let me see your face!" Eda turns to Mom and uncovers her mouth, which is already swelling and bloody. Mom says, "Go wash up, and when you come back, redo your work. That handwriting of yours is disgusting! And remember, if anyone asks what happened, you say that you fell down. Understand, you stupid girl?" Mom shakes her finger at Eda.

Ed looks scared, and I cry openly. It always makes me sad to see Ed or Eda cry with that look of fear they so often have. Ed tucks his chin to his chest and wraps his hands around his head, so Mom cannot pull his ears or slap him.

"Shut up, Ariana! Stop your damn crying!"

But I can't stop, so I slip under the table. When Eda comes back, I crawl toward Eda's dangling feet, grabbing her leg for safety. From under the table, I can see rage in Mom's eyes.

She gets up, snatches her crocheting, and slaps Eda again, then shakes her finger at us, screaming like a madwoman, "To hell with all of you *and* your homework!" and stomps out of the room to the courtyard.

After a few seconds, I scoot out from under the table. "Eda, don't cry," I console her, rubbing her arm.

Ed tilts his head in Mom's direction and reminds us, "She's an *esh*."

Eda and I giggle. We both know he shouldn't be calling her a donkey. After all, she is our mother . . . but it feels good to hear him say it.

Eda chides, "If Mom hears you, we are dead meat!"

The three of us share broken smiles.

Watermelons

AT THE AGE OF FIVE, I begin first grade. All schools start at the first of fall, so the mornings are chilly, and as the day goes on, it warms up until the evening cools. I can hardly wait! Ed, Eda, and I have new school uniforms and shoes. My uniform looks just like Eda's. It's a navy-blue dress with long sleeves, white collar, and a bunch of buttons down the front. Two pockets adorn each side and it falls below the knees. Eda and I wear long white stockings. A big white bow crowns my ponytail; a headband frames her face and long, silky hair cascades down her back.

Ed's uniform consists of a short jacket and dark pants. We each carry book bags to hold our school supplies. My bag is brand new, while Ed's and Eda's are left over from last year.

Eda had told me we'd all share one building, the same lunch time, and even recess. I'm pretty scared to be with all the big kids. Thank goodness I have Ed and Eda. Together, we walk the mile-long trek.

"Eda," I ask. "How many days do we go to school?"

"I told you, Ariana. We have school five and a half days."

"Can we play at recess?"

"Yes, we can play, but you mustn't misbehave or get into a fight, or the assistant principal, Mr. Morady, who is always outside in the yard, will get mad."

"The one who punished Ed last year?"

"Yes. He is so mean."

"I don't like him, Eda."

"Believe me. No one does."

Ed, who is walking ahead of us swinging his black book bag, turns around and says, "He is a big *esh*! When I'm older, I will punch him in the nose."

Eda laughs. "You're right, Ed. He is a big donkey."

Finally, we arrive at school and enter through the open iron gate. The schoolyard is huge! Kids scurry about everywhere while I hold onto Eda's hand. The three of us walk toward the steep stairs and make our way to the main building. Ed disappears, and Eda walks me to my classroom. She tells me to stay there, instructing me not to move or talk. It's so big! The room has lots of wooden benches in it. Hanging on the walls are some pictures of fruits and vegetables, as well as alphabet letters and numbers.

Feeling a little lost, I stand in the middle of the room, staring at the boys and girls, none of whom I know. I notice a long blackboard lining the wall with pieces of white chalk and a dirty rag lying on its ledge. In front of that wall sits a big wooden desk and folding chair, with a kerosene heater perched at the end.

I nearly come out of my skin when I hear a loud bell ring. Then a tall lady with books in her arms and a handbag over her shoulder walks into the room. She has long, wavy black hair. Her eyes are outlined in dark makeup and she wears bright red lipstick. As she walks in, she announces, "I am your teacher, and my name is Miss Houma. Find a place and sit quietly."

I sit in the first empty spot I can find. Next to me is a chubby girl, bigger than Eda. She has messy, short, curly hair, and I notice she is drooling like a baby. Her eyes are large and puffy, and she is making noises that are foreign to me.

"Be quiet!" Miss Houma shouts as she hits her desk with a wooden ruler.

She then instructs us that when we enter her classroom, we must do so in silence. She commands us to sit at our spot with our clean, white handkerchief folded on our desk. Our palms are to be facing down on the desk, so she can check for clean hands and trimmed fingernails. We also must have our notebook, black pencil, sharpener, eraser, and a ruler on the desk arranged just so.

The girl next to me continues to make noises. Her saliva is running down her chin and onto her clothes. I want to help the girl with whom I share a bench, but I'm scared. Then Miss Houma approaches me, asking for my name.

I turn to her, afraid to talk, but I whisper, "Ariana."

She firmly asks, "Ariana what? Do you have a last name?"

"Yes, I do."

"Well, what is it?" she demands.

I whisper, "Mikaelian."

"Oh, so you are a Christian?"

I had never been asked this, but I knew it was true. I wasn't sure if this was the answer she wanted, but I timidly answer, "Yes."

She kind of smiles at me, then looks at the girl sitting next to me. "What is your name?" Miss Houma asks.

The girl just makes some unclear noises. Miss Houma looks at her with raised eyebrows.

"She's mute and retarded!" a boy from the back row blurts out.

Everyone in the class gasps and there is silence.

"Who was that?" Miss Houma demands.

The boy stands up, admitting, "It was me, ma'am."

"Well, next time, ask for permission to talk. By the way, how do you know?"

"Well, miss, she lives down the street from me, and she is even older than my second-grade brother. She never could talk, at least that's what her mom told my mom."

Miss Houma says, "Enough. You can sit down now."

Silence fills the room. I keep looking at the girl. I'd like to help her clean her face and mouth, but I am hesitant.

Miss Houma keeps walking to the next student and the next, until she's gotten everyone's name in her book. With her back to the blackboard, she stands in front of the class and begins to tell us we must obey the rules, listen to her carefully, and follow her directions, or we will be punished.

Here we go, again. Just another place, another person I have to obey.

Miss Houma keeps talking. Right then and there, I decide that even if I don't understand something she says, I'm not going to ask her anything or say anything. Who knows? If I don't obey, she'll probably hit me, just like Mom.

***

It doesn't take long for me to taste punishment in school, as I'd suspected. We all got assigned a project to do at home, and mine was to draw fruits and vegetables. Unfortunately, I'm not very good at drawing, so Eda comes to my rescue. She draws pictures of some watermelons, but they are not the kind Miss Houma likes.

"What the heck is this? You call these watermelons? You lazy, stupid girl!" And with the side of her wooden ruler, she hits the palms of my hands so hard and for so long, they begin to bleed. In panic and pain, the silence of the classroom engulfs me. The boys and girls sitting near me look terrorized and are pinned to their seats, grateful it's not them being punished.

My bloody hands burn. I make them into fists and hope the pain will go away. Tears cover my face, yet I try to follow Miss Houma's instruction. The bell rings for recess, and everyone leaves in a rush. I follow. Outside the door, I spot Eda waiting for me. She immediately notices the tears in my eyes and asks, "What happened?"

I show her my palms.

"Did your teacher do this?"

I nod my head.

"Ariana, she's crazy! Come on. Let's go to the water fountain, so I can wash your hands." Eda leads me there and gingerly takes both my wrists and holds my palms under the water to wash my wounds.

"We need to get you some bandages."

"But Eda, my teacher will get mad." ·

"Don't worry. We are going to the nice assistant principal."

When we arrive at the office, Eda asks for bandages. The lady also gives her a napkin to dry my hands. Once my sister has covered my hands, she tells me, "Ariana, try not to think about it. We'll be going home very soon." She kisses my head.

With that, I am able to make it through the school day.

***

On our way home, I ask Eda, "Do you think Mom will get mad at me?"

"I don't know, Ariana." She keeps her eyes straight ahead so I can't tell what she is thinking.

"What about Papa? Will he be mad?"

"Papa? Oh, no. He might get upset at your teacher, but not you."

Once we get home, Eda tells Mom all about my punishment.

"Come *here*, Ariana," Mom orders.

"It wasn't my fault, Mom," I say with my voice choked up. "My teacher didn't like the watermelons that Eda drew for me, so she hit me with her ruler."

"Let me see your hands," Mom demands. To our surprise, she exclaims, "Is your teacher crazy!?"

After she examines my palms, she puts medicine on them and freshly wraps them with white gauze. "Now change your clothes. I will go to the school tomorrow."

***

The next day, I knew Mom had complained to the principal. She told Papa and every neighbor how she had let the principal have it. Every time she told the story, the more praise and attention she received. Mom was so proud. I could see it in her face. Did my punishment bring her this feeling?

Heavy snow covers the ground. With a wooden shovel, Mom cleans a walkway to the entry door. When she's tired, she orders Ed to push the rest of the snow to the back side of the yard.

The roofs of most houses are made with a mixture of clay and straw. If the snow is not cleared, its weight will collapse the roof. Because this happened to part of our roof once, Mom is very cautious. She hires workers, who are bundled up and walking the streets during this time of the year yelling, "Roof shovelers!" They come and shovel the snow, dumping it in the yard. Then they push it to one side of the yard into a pile.

Today, the snow is extremely heavy. School is out, and Ed, Eda, and I are home. But I've been home since yesterday. I don't feel good, my throat hurts, and I'm coughing a lot.

"Mom, I'm cold, and my chest hurts."

"Here," she replies and hands me a little pink pill. "Chew on this. It will make you feel better."

"Why is it pink, Mom?"

"This aspirin is for children. The white ones are for adults."

I chew and try to swallow, but it's so hard. My throat feels so big inside. Then Mom touches my forehead and says, "You are burning up."

I've been sick before, but never like this. Near the kerosene heater, Mom makes a bed on the floor.

"Eda, go get the thermometer from the chest of drawers in my room. It's in the top drawer," Mom orders.

Mom brings a pot of water and places it on the heater. She then adds eucalyptus leaves, which release an aroma when the water gets hot. Mom says, "This will sanitize the air and help you breathe better."

Eda returns with the thermometer and hands it to me.

"Put it under your tongue, Ariana," Mom says. "And don't squeeze it with your teeth. If it breaks, the mercury will get into your mouth and kill you."

I hold the stick carefully under my tongue for at least a minute.

"Okay, give it to me now." She holds it up to the light and reads, "Forty [this is Celsius, so my temperature was 104F]. Your fever is very high." She leaves to go to the kitchen and returns with a few wet towels, putting one on my forehead and wrapping my feet with the other. "Try to sleep, Ariana. The medicine I gave you will help."

For the rest of the day, I lie down. I don't feel like getting up or eating. Sometimes when I cough a lot, Mom makes me hot tea with honey. When I sit up to drink, I see it's getting dark outside and still snowing. Exhausted, I fall back to sleep.

I wake up with Mom sitting beside me. I have the shivers, and a cold towel is on my forehead. I keep coughing. It's so hard to breathe.

"Get up, Ariana. Let me change your nightgown. I have to take you to the hospital." Mom helps me into my clothes. I feel very dizzy and tired.

The next thing I know, Mom and I are standing in the main street. It's so cold and no one is around. I hold Mom's hand and rest my head on her hip. I stare up at the dark sky; dropping snowflakes look like butterflies under the streetlights. They sit on my face, and it feels good.

"Mom, I'm tired."

"I know you are, Ariana. Hopefully a taxi will pass by very soon."

Before long, a car pulls up beside us and rolls down the window. The lady driver asks, "Where are you going, ma'am?"

"My daughter is burning up with fever. I need to get her to the hospital," Mom answers.

"Hurry up and get in the car. I am a nurse. That's where I'm going."

We both climb inside, and as soon as Mom and I are settled, I fall asleep. When I open my eyes, I'm lying in a big bed with white sheets. The lady nurse is standing near me, next to a man in a long white coat. He listens to my chest and says, "Hi, pretty girl. Can you tell me where it hurts?"

I point to my throat and then to my chest. He examines me and says, "Open your mouth and say 'Ahhh.'"

As I do, he pushes down my tongue with a metal stick, making me gag.

"Okay," he says. "You did good."

Then he talks to Mom and to the nurse. Soon, the nurse comes over to me with a needle in her hand. "Turn over on your tummy. I'm going to give you a shot. Be a big girl, it's just gonna hurt a little bit."

Before I know it, I've got a shot in my booty! "Ouch!"

She helps me sit up and pats me on the shoulder as I fight back tears. The doctor hands Mom a bottle of medicine and says, "Give this to her until it is all gone. I'm glad you brought her here."

"Of course, Doctor. I had to. My husband is never home. I am the one stuck with the kids," Mom complains.

"She will be fine," the doctor says, walking away.

The nurse then leads us to the front of the hospital and asks the doorman to get us a taxi while we wait inside.

"Thank you so much," Mom says. "You may be a nurse, but tonight, you have been an angel to us."

"That's kind of you, ma'am," she answers. "Go home, rest, and *you*, little girl, will be fine soon," she says as she caresses my hair.

***

For the next few days, I stay home, mostly in bed. But as soon as Ed and Eda come home, I get up, excited to see them. Eda hugs me and says, "Are you feeling better?"

"Yes, my throat doesn't hurt as much," I reply.

"That's good. I don't like it when you're sick." She hugs me tight again and says, "Now close your eyes. I have a surprise for you."

I do as she asks. "Now open your eyes."

Eda is holding a book in front of me. I say, "Oh, Eda, is this for me?" The picture on the cover shows a little girl in raggedy clothes, sitting on a street corner on a cold, snowy night.

"Yes, it is!" Eda reads the title to me. *"The Little Match Girl* by Hans Christian Andersen."

I reach for the book, then flip through the pretty pictures, over and over again. *I can't believe it. My very first book.*

Eda smiles and says, "I bought it with my money. It will keep you busy, Ariana."

"Throwing your father's money away again," Mom remarks. "Eda, go to the kitchen and bring us a tray of snacks."

I don't feel like eating, but I drink the tea with one hand, while the other sits on top of my new book.

***

Life soon goes back to normal— school, homework, and regular scoldings. Sometimes, I wish I'd get sick more often, since that's the only time Mom is nice.

Yellow Tin

THE SNOW ON THE GROUND is melting—no more slippery roads, no more falling, no more shivering in the cold on our way to school.

Instead, the trees are blooming and the temperature is rising. Since we will have about two weeks of school holiday, every student is ecstatic. This break is also the traditional Persian New Year, *Norooz*. The entire country celebrates, so all our Persian friends and neighbors buy new clothes, cook their best dishes, and visit family and friends. In my house, however, there is none of this. Our culture is different. As Armenians, we celebrate Christmas and the New Year on the first of January.

But the excitement for Ed, Eda, and me doesn't last long. Not only must we obey Mom's rules, but now we are loaded with extra homework during the break. We despise doing it since Mom is always there to check it. Our teachers want to make sure we don't forget what we've learned so far during the year, so they load us up with work. For Ed and Eda, they have to copy their literature and history books and write ten essays each. And for me, since I'm still in first grade, I have lots of vocabulary words to write and math problems to solve.

On the first day of our break, Ed, Eda, and I wake up to Mom's loud voice. "Get up! How long are you going to stay in bed? It's already seven o'clock! If you're not in the kitchen in five minutes, there will be no breakfast."

The three of us jump out of bed, quickly wash up, and change from our pajamas to our house clothes. You see, in my house, we are never allowed to oversleep or spend the day in our pajamas. My house is a boot camp, and my mom is the staff sergeant. She believes if my siblings and I aren't being yelled at or punished, we won't grow up to be decent people.

We quietly tiptoe to the kitchen to have our breakfast. We know better than to talk to one another. In silence, we gather our plates of cheese, pita bread, honey, and a cup of tea. We sit at the table on wooden chairs that I really like. They have flowers carved into the seats and backs. When I run my fingers over the pattern, it kind of tickles my hands. When we sit on them, they make squeaky noises, and when I move, the chair wiggles, making Mom angry.

As I am about to take a piece of cheese, my chair moves, and my foot accidentally touches one of the legs of the table, causing Ed to spill his tea.

Mom whips around, yelling, "Look what you've done! You're all worthless kids!" She snatches each of our breakfast plates one by one and throws them against the kitchen wall.

I try to hide behind Eda, and Ed scurries under the table.

"What are you sheltering Ariana for?" Mom yells at Eda. For this, Eda gets slapped, again and again.

"Mom, please!" I beg, my voice choked up in my throat. "Please Mom, dear Mom, I didn't mean for this to happen. I swear to you. I didn't do it on purpose. It was an accident."

"Oh, so it was you?" She grabs my hair and yanks me to the side, slapping my face. "You unruly and cursed little slut."

I really don't know what she means by "slut," but she often calls me this. I *know* it's not a good thing.

Mom lets go of my ponytail, grabs me by the ear, and twists it so hard, it gets hot and hurts. I hold onto her hand and beg her to stop.

"Will you do it again? Will you?"

"No, no, Mom. I will never. Please . . ." I sob irrepressibly.

Finally, she releases me. Frightened, the three of us leave the kitchen. Eda puts her hand on my shoulder as we follow Ed to the living room. Sad and uncertain, we sit quietly on the floor in a corner of the room. We are still hungry, too, but what we want most is for Mom to calm down and not be angry. I don't know how long we sit there doing nothing. I think Ed and Eda are terrified, just like me. I count the shapes and flowers woven on the rug, and every so often, Ed gets up and goes to the door.

Finally, Eda tells him, "Sit down or Mom will come and get you."

"But I have to pee! I can't hold it anymore!"

"Okay, go quickly. Maybe Mom won't find out," Eda whispers, eyes darting between Ed and the door, listening intently.

Ed slowly opens the door, looking quickly toward the kitchen, and runs to the bathroom. In a flash, he comes back, breathless. "Did she see I was gone?"

"No, but we have to be very quiet so she won't lose her temper again," Eda warns.

"Why does she keep hitting us? Are we bad children, Eda?" I ask timidly.

She shrugs her shoulders. "I guess. I don't know."

Ed says, "We aren't bad. She's crazy. I bet none of our cousins get punished like we do."

"You know," I say, "once I asked cousin Nina if her mom hits her. She said, 'Not really. Sometimes when I do something bad, she slaps my hand, but it doesn't even hurt.'"

"Of course not. No one gets it like us," Ed adds.

I sigh. "I wish Papa was here."

Mom comes to the living room a few times to check on us. Each time, she scolds, "See? You stupid kids! Until you are punished, you won't be quiet and obedient!"

Every time she leaves the room, we sit there, frightened and hungry. Mom eventually walks out of the house, warning, "If you misbehave while I am gone, I will kill you all."

***

It must be afternoon by now. I cry, "Eda, aren't you hungry? My tummy hurts."

"I'm starving!" Ed announces. "Let's go to the kitchen and grab something to eat while the monster is gone!"

"Be quiet, *geesh*! Mom might hear you!" Eda whispers loudly.

"She isn't even home. Plus, *she's* the crazy one," Ed replies in a normal voice.

"Well, she might just appear. You know how she is."

"I don't care. I'm going to find something to eat," he insists.

I stand up, look at Eda, and urge, "Let's go."

The three of us enter our kitchen, like bandits searching for food, hoping to find something Mom won't miss.

Ed comes up with a splendid idea. "I know, I know! Let's eat the *nazook*! I'm sure she didn't count them."

We all walk to Mom's bedroom with hesitancy. Ed goes toward the shelving in the corner of the room that's hidden behind a floral curtain to find the big yellow tin.

"Ed, bring me a knife," Eda says.

"Hold on!" In a flash, he's back. "Here, let me do it." He kneels in front of the tin. I watch his moves closely. He sticks the flat side of the knife under the edge of the lid and pops it open.

I am so proud of him. "Good job, Ed!"

Eda grabs a few *nazook* and puts them in her skirt, closes the lid, and pushes back the tin.

"Make sure it's in the right place and the curtain is closed all the way," Eda instructs.

"I got it!" Ed runs to the kitchen to put back the knife.

We hurry back to the living room. Eda sits on the floor, opens her skirt, and spreads it. Ed and I sit close to her, each grabbing a *nazook* and nibbling just a little. It takes everything in us not to gulp down the scrumptious, buttery shortbread in one bite.

The three of us finish our first *nazook* within seconds, making sure we hold our hands over Eda's skirt so the crumbs fall only there. We look at each other, knowing we want more. After two *nazook* each, Eda says, "I hope Mom doesn't feed us dinner when she comes home."

"To punish us, she won't," Ed replies. "Let's have another one!"

But I can't eat any more, so I give mine to Ed. After they are finished, Eda carefully grabs the corners of her skirt and brings them together.

"Ed, open the door." Eda walks to the yard, with Ed and me following. Behind the evergreen, she carefully shakes her skirt, then we quickly return to the living room.

It isn't long before Mom comes home. We hear her steps going straight to the kitchen.

As we look at each other with tension, I say, "Eda, is Mom going to bring us food?"

Eda answers, "I hope not."

"*I'm* still hungry," Ed says.

I reply, "Not me."

Just then, Mom enters the room with a tray full of baloney sandwiches. All three of us take one as Mom commands. Ed eats his, while Eda and I just nibble on ours. With hearts pounding in our chests, we hope we didn't leave any trace of our sneaky snacking.

Words of Comfort

NOROOZ IS STILL GOING ON, as is our homework. Every day after lunch, it is our "mandatory" nap time.

"Go get your pillows and blankets, and get ready for nap time," Mom says firmly. Pointing at Ed and Eda, she warns, "If you are not sleeping, you'd better be quiet. You hear me?"

Ed and Eda nod.

"But Mom, I'm not tired," I reply.

"What did you say?" Mom dares me.

"Nothing, Mom," I whisper.

"Now shut up and lay down."

I do as I am told and lie next to Mom. Ed sleeps on the other side of her. I see Mom place the fly swatter above her pillow. It's so hard not to move, so I grab my bangs and twist them around my pointer finger until my hand is tired. I want to get up so badly. I look over at Ed, who is asleep. Eda, on the other side of the room, quietly lays an old rag on the floor, setting up her canvas and brushes Mom had allowed her to buy with her allowance. She noiselessly puts the canvas against the wall and puts a few drops of oil paint on the wooden palette.

I want to watch Eda paint. Carefully, I push my blanket away, turn, and as I'm about to crawl, I hear Mom. "You little devil. Where do you think you're going?" Instantaneously, the bright yellow fly swatter lands on my thigh. "Didn't I tell you not to move?"

I place my hand on my thigh as tears course down my face. I close my eyes.

"I bet you can sleep now," Mom says as she turns her back to me. "And you over there. You think you're an artist? You are a worthless, stupid girl."

I fall asleep.

***

After the peaceless nap, Mom lets us venture outside to play. In the corner of our yard sits a red bicycle. It has been handed down to Ed and Eda, but as long as I remember, they never got to ride it. Not only does it have a flat tire, but its chain is also broken. Every time I see the bike, I wish Papa could fix it, so I can ride my own. I don't like begging Hamlet to take turns on his.

Other than the bicycle, I have an old, handed-down doll, minus hair and clothes. Since my cousin Annie hit my doll's head on the floor, she doesn't even have eyes.

Ed's toys aren't any better than mine. He has a homemade slingshot and a red-striped, cheap plastic ball, which caves in if it's hit too hard. Still, he throws it against the wall. Eda begs him to stop since she knows it will anger Mom, but Ed pays no attention to her.

As the words leave her mouth, the ball hits one of Mom's clay flower pots, shattering it to pieces.

All three of us panic. I stand still with my doll in one hand. Ed grabs the ball and keeps it under one arm, attempting to cover it with his other. His eyebrows are scrunched, not wanting to give himself away.

Eda rushes to pick up the broken pieces, hoping Mom won't notice. Eda's like that, always trying to cover up for us. "*Esh*! I told you to be careful! Don't just stand there, come and help me!"

Little did we know that Mom had heard the shattering. She comes storming to the yard, swearing and shaking her finger at us.

"I'm going to kill you! I'm gonna beat you so bad you won't be able to move! Whose fault is it?"

I don't know what to do. With panic in my voice, I plead, "Mom, I didn't do it. Mom, please don't hurt me!" As I slowly step backward, she slaps me so hard, my face goes numb.

She stomps over to Eda and grabs her arm, shoving her into a corner. "Who was it? Who broke the flower pot?" she demands as she looks down at the broken pieces. "Which one of you did this?"

Ed, shivering, standing against the wall, has tears flooding his face and snot running from his nose. With a weak voice, he squeaks, "Mom, I didn't mean to break it. Mom, please! Please don't hurt me!"

Ed begs for mercy as Mom reaches for him. She grabs him by the neck and slaps him hard across the face. His pale skin now reveals a crimson handprint. Mom grabs the thick, heavy water hose with a golden nozzle on one end, holds the hose in the middle, so it's free to swing in the air, and begins to beat my brother with it.

Our landlord must have heard the commotion and comes running to Ed's rescue. As soon as Mom sees him, her violence stops and she sinks to the ground.

"Liz, calm down! What is going on?" he asks, visibly shaken.

Eda rushes to Ed and takes his hand. He gasps for breath and his whole body trembles. The lashings have left his arms and legs raw, bruised, and bloody. It hurts me to see him in pain.

Eda takes him inside the house, but I stand frozen in the yard. Mom, who is still sitting on the ground, leans against the red brick wall, crying and hitting herself on her legs. I've seen her do this before. Totally out of control, hysterical, she cannot speak.

Mr. Arman yells in the direction of his house, "Mary, can you get some of those valerian calming drops for Liz?"

Mrs. Mary soon comes with a small glass and hands it to Mom. "Drink it," she says, and Mom does.

"Okay, now tell me what happened that has made you so upset," our landlord urges her.

"Oh, Mr. Arman, you have no idea how miserable they make me. Especially that boy! He just broke my flower pot!" Mom shouts.

Mrs. Mary chastises, "That isn't a good enough reason for you to hit him the way you did. He is covered in blood and bruises! You hurt that child because of a broken pot?" Her voice is tense and frown lines form.

Mr. Arman stares her down and says firmly, "Liz, you must control your anger."

Mom stops sniveling and replies, "I can't help it when they are so unruly." She tilts her head back and closes her eyes.

Eda comes out, takes my hand, and we walk inside the house together. There is a deep silence as our sadness sinks into the paint on the walls. None of our uncles or aunties knows how badly we get punished. We all feel trapped with nowhere to go.

As we hold onto each other, the three of us hide our pain and we forget. Forget and wait for Papa to come home.

***

A few fear-filled days later, Papa arrives. Eda and I run to him and I do my usual thing, jump into his embrace and smell his familiar scent. I don't ever want to let him go.

"Well, well, how are my beautiful girls?" As he leads us inside, he spots Ed sitting on a wooden chair with a royal blue seat cover, doing his homework. Immediately, Papa's grin turns upside down.

"Ed, are those bruises on your face? And your arms? Have you been in a fist fight?"

Ed quietly weeps; his lips quiver. He cannot make eye contact with Papa.

I tap on Papa's back. "No, Papa, Mom did it. She was so mad at Ed, she hit him with the garden hose! Papa, I was so scared. You know, we were playing, and Ed kicked his ball and it hit the flower pot. That's all he did, Papa! Even Mrs. Mary told Mom she shouldn't have hit Ed like she did!" I know Mom is preparing food in the kitchen, so I get to tell my story without her hearing.

Papa caresses my hair and says, "Ariana, you know your mother loves you, Ed, and Eda very much, and if she punishes you, it's not because she is mean. It's not her fault. She is a nervous woman who cannot control her anger."

"But Papa, can't you stop her?"

He looks down and murmurs, "I wish I could."

So, we are getting punished because Mom doesn't know how to control her anger? I listen to Papa, but somehow his words don't comfort me. I am terrified Mom will do this again, perhaps to *me* next time.

1969–1972
The Forbidden Graveyard

AS EASTER DRAWS NEAR, the weather is beautiful with crisp, sunny days. All the trees and rose bushes have bloomed. Mom has planted a new honeysuckle bush next to the evergreen tree. Its sweet aroma fills the air. Eda and I pick some of the small yellow and white blossoms, pull the center out, and lick the end of it. There's barely a drop of sweetness on it. I guess that's why it's called honeysuckle?

Mom announces our annual family reunion is coming. I'm so excited! An entire day of play, good food, *nazook*, and best of all, we get to go to the cemetery!

Finally, my cousins Nina, Freddy, and Rafael, along with my aunties, arrive at our house for lunch. Everyone is dressed in their new Easter outfits and shiny shoes. Eda and I have on our new white dresses embroidered by Mom with pastel flowers; Ed wears his new khaki pants with a blue button-down shirt. We all know that before we can go to play, we must change into different clothes. And because we were promised we could go outside once we were done eating, we can't eat fast enough.

As soon as it's time to take off, Mom gives Eda a clay container filled with water and each of us a *nazook*. When Mom isn't looking, we steal more *nazook* and hide them in our pockets.

Mom stops us to lecture, with her forefinger pointing to each one in turn. "Do *not* go to the cemetery and bother the mortician."

"Yes, Mom," Ed answers, as my cousins and I nod in unison.

We all line up behind Ed to head out to our secret destination.

As we are leaving, Mom sternly warns, "Come home before dark."

Across the green metal bridge, beyond the uphill dirt road, the graveyard stretches out before us. At first, we all run, then slow down, breathless. Ed and Rafael drag a stick along behind them, kicking up dust clouds. Every once in a while, Nina, Freddy, and I bend down to pick up a handful of pebbles and throw them around to each other. We trudge over dirt, rocks, and gravel. At one point, Freddy stumbles and falls, but quickly gets back on his feet, wipes his nose, and runs to keep up with the pack.

Eda points at the big iron gate painted a yellowish-green with an old faded sign hanging above it. "Hassan-Abad Cemetery."

For a second, we hesitate, then, as one large mass, silently enter. We all know it is said that the mortician's wife is a crazy lady who steals wandering children . . . and buries them alive!

All is quiet, except for the occasional caw from a crow as it lands on a tombstone. We approach unorganized rows of graves. Some have headstones, others have ledger markers, many are cracked or chipped with overgrown weeds and thorny cacti between them. Most hold a framed photograph of the deceased.

Nina and I hold hands as we follow along behind Ed and Rafael. Eda and Freddy are behind us, looking at a grave.

"Nina, why are these pictures so scary?" I ask.

"I don't know, Ariana, but they sure scare me, too."

Ed hears us and says, "You idiots! That's because they take the pictures after the person is dead!"

Nina starts to cry and runs to Eda.

"Shut up, Ed," Eda scolds.

Rafael and Ed have a good laugh, walking away.

A few minutes later, Nina, Eda, Freddy, and I notice Ed farther ahead, holding up a stick and pointing at something. With curiosity, we run to him. Ed gestures for us to sit down. As he and Rafael hide behind a headstone, Nina and I squat down, hoping no one can see us. Freddy, who is even more scared than we are, keeps running back and forth between Ed and Rafael, and Nina and me. Eda walks in Ed's direction to see what he was pointing at.

"What do you see, Eda?" I ask.

Before Eda can answer, Rafael jumps in front of us saying all spooky-like, "It's a zombie!"

Ed corrects him. "No, it's the crazy lady, and she's drowning somebody in a pool!"

"No, she's not," Eda assures all of us. "She's washing clothes. Come on out, you guys!"

We all get up and go to where Eda is standing. There, in the lower section of the cemetery, is a clam —a house made of clay and straw— belonging to the mortician. In front of it is a small pool where the crazy lady, with messy hair and a white *chadour* wrapped around her waist, is kneeling, holding something in the water, then pulls it out. Eda is right! She *is* washing clothes.

Even though we've been here before, each adventure at the cemetery feels like the very first time. We go from one grave to another, trying to read the name carved on each ledger marker. Eda does the math to figure out how old the person was.

A short time later, Ed declares, "Time to rest and eat our snack."

All agree wholeheartedly. With hungry anticipation, we each choose a ledger marker to sit on. First, we rub our hands over the stone to wipe the dirt and pebbles off, then dust our hands on our clothes.

"Okay, hand me the *nazook* so I can divide them," Eda says, giving each one of us our share. With joy, we indulge in our snack as Eda passes the clay container around for us to drink water. "Here, drink some water, but be careful not to drop the container. If it breaks, my mom *won't* be happy,"

Still sitting on the grave, Nina and I run our fingers over the dusty areas, pretending the lines are pictures of a house and flowers. Ed and Rafael are chasing Freddy, when Eda calls out, "Hey, guys! It's getting dark. Hurry up, we have to leave!"

We all reluctantly obey and line up behind Ed, just the way we did before. Nina and I once again hold hands and swing them back and forth.

As we head for home, Rafael says in a loud voice, "Hey, listen up! Stay close, now that the sun is going down. This reminds me of the last time Ed and I were here and something really scary happened to us. That day, when we came to the cemetery, we got lost. Before we knew it, we had fallen into a grave! From down inside, we could hear the voices of the rising dead. We closed our eyes and prayed to God for our dear lives. I even had to cover Ed's mouth to keep him quiet. After what seemed like hours, we heard footsteps coming closer. First, I thought it was the mortician's wife, but then I wondered if it might be the walking dead! Ed and I held on to each other, hunkered down, until I felt a hand on my head. Scared to death, I peeked through my fingers, not knowing what I would see."

Rafael gets quiet. We all stop walking. I know I'm scared, and I can see Nina's and Freddy's eyes frozen wide with fear.

"What was it?" I ask anxiously.

Rafael takes a deep breath and in a loud voice says, "It was . . ."

"Well, *what was it*, Rafael?" I ask again.

"A zombie!" Rafael shouts.

Nina and I run to Eda, but Freddy keeps screaming and starts to run away.

Eda admonishes, "Shut up, Rafael! Stop lying."

"Stop running, Freddy!" Ed yells and takes off after him.

He doesn't slow down a bit, so we all follow suit. As he reaches the top of the hill, his foot slips, he loses his balance, and he tumbles all the way down to the bottom. We rush over to him.

Eda calls out, "Freddy, Freddy!" She pulls Nina and me along with her. Panic is written all over her face. I know she's thinking the worst.

Ed is the first one to get to him. Poor Freddy is all bloody, with open wounds on his head, arms, and legs. Thank God, he is conscious. We have nothing with us to help clean him up, but Eda thinks to wash his wounds with water from the clay pot. She gingerly rinses the dirt away, then turns to me and says, "Ariana, take the container, and be careful not to drop it."

I hold the pot real tight to my chest and follow Eda, who's giving Freddy a piggyback ride home.

Freddy's cries get the attention of Mom and Auntie Helen as we approach the house. When they see poor Freddy's bloody face, I know they are scared to death. Auntie Helen, Freddy's mom, picks him up and sets him on the table.

"Liz, what should I do?" she cries helplessly.

"Don't worry, Helen, I'll get what you need." Mom hurries off and returns quickly with a first aid kit, opens it, and pulls out gauze and medicine to help Auntie Helen clean up Freddy. Together, they doctor his wounds and stop the bleeding.

Auntie fingers his hair and consoles him. "My little boy, you are so lucky to be alive." She hugs him and tenderly kisses his head. "I will take care of you, and you will be fine, *Baless*."

I'm standing near Auntie Helen, watching her lovingly care for Freddy, and I wonder why Mom never says things like that to us.

I am startled back to the moment when Mom's yelling draws my attention. "How could you let Freddy get hurt? You are so irresponsible! What if something more serious had happened to him?" Mom belittles Ed and Eda. "Did you go to the cemetery again? I told you not to go to there! Why must you disobey me, you unruly children?"

Mom pulls Ed's ear so hard it makes him weep. With his palm, he covers Mom's hand of fury, trying to make her stop.

Auntie Janet steps in. "It's okay, Liz. It must have been an accident. They are only kids. Let him go. By the way, you shouldn't get upset over little things. It's not good for the baby."

Mom touches her belly and nods her head in agreement. "These kids won't let me relax for a moment."

That's when I notice a bump underneath Mom's floral sundress. I walk over to touch it. "Is there a baby in there?"

"Shut up! It's none of your business, nosy!"

Eda pulls me away and says, "There is a baby, but we must not talk about it. It's not polite, nor is it proper for children's conversation."

I obey Eda, but I still have a thousand questions in my mind.

The rest of the night is a blur. My uncles come for dinner, and I'm already missing my cousins. I wish they could stay forever.

High-Heeled Shoes

ONE DAY, LATE IN THE SUMMER, Papa takes Mom somewhere and Ed, Eda, and I stay home. We soon learn Mom is in the hospital, and we now have a little baby brother.

Early the next morning, Papa tells me I get to go to the hospital with him to visit Mom and meet the baby. I can't wait!

Eda chooses my white tights, pleated blue skirt, and white blouse. As I push my feet into my old maroon shoes, Eda brushes my hair and puts it in a ponytail. Papa and I leave and make our way to the main thoroughfare. I know we'll go to the bus station, but Papa has a surprise for me first.

As we approach the shoe store, Papa stops and gestures at the shoes behind the window. "My pretty girl, which shoes would you like to have?"

In one glance, I spot the most beautiful pair of shoes I've ever seen. "Those, Papa, those!" I point at some black high-heeled shoes.

Holding Papa's hand, I rush inside the store. In disbelief, I ask, "Papa, really? You'll buy me these shoes?"

"Of course, *Baless*," he says lovingly.

"Which ones, sir?" the clerk asks.

Papa points, replying, "The black high-heeled shoes."

The clerk says, "The ones with a two-centimeter heel?"

Papa grins. "Yes, those."

"Do you know what size?" the clerk asks.

Papa looks at me, puzzled, smiling coyly. "No, I have no clue."

"No problem." The clerk produces a weird-looking metal ruler and puts my foot on it. "Okay, stand still and relax your toes. Good! Now you can step back." The clerk memorizes the size, then starts toward a black curtain at the back of the store, but stops abruptly, turns to Papa, and says matter-of-factly, "Size four and a half."

In a matter of minutes, the clerk returns with a few shoe boxes stacked on his arms. "I brought a couple of them just in case one doesn't fit."

I can't wait to try them on! I slide my right foot, then the left, into my new pair of shoes. "Papa, look! They fit me!"

He seems as happy as I do. "They sure look nice, but tell me something. Can you wiggle your toes?"

I move my toes in my new shoes. "Yes, Papa, yes!" Ecstatic, I look at Papa and still can't believe he is buying me these shoes. He has *never* gotten me, my sister, or my brother anything besides the souvenirs he brings home from the different cities to which he travels. Mom's always the one who takes us shopping.

Wearing my new high-heeled shoes, I head with Papa to catch the bus. I hate to admit it, but I am much more excited about my brand-new black shoes than I am about my baby brother!

At the bus station, we have to wait for the big red double-decker bus to arrive. It's so much fun to sit in the upper deck! Ed always tells me the second level of the bus doesn't have a driver and makes me believe it's magical.

My strong papa picks me up with one arm and carries me up the stairs. It is crowded, dirty, and smells gross. The red plastic covers on some of the seats are torn and the stuffing is even coming out, but it feels so good sitting next to Papa. I dangle my feet, check my new shoes, and rest my head on his arm. Every few minutes, I scoot closer to the window and look outside. I see the grocers selling fresh walnuts and roasted corn on the cob from their stands, clapping to draw the pedestrians' attention to their merchandise, and the sidewalk is busy with women holding their children's hands as they shop. The view is mesmerizing.

Sometimes, when Mom takes us places on the bus, scary things happen. People yell bad words at each other and strangers touch women. Mom gets furious when that happens to her.

But today, the ride is without incident. The bus driver soon pulls over, and Papa gently taps my shoulder. We get off near a big building that looks different from other places.

"Look, Papa! All these walls are shiny!"

"Yes, that's marble, not brick like all the others."

After a short walk, we enter the big building. Inside, it is quiet and it smells funny. I notice a lady mopping the floor. Papa asks her where we need to go to find my baby brother. He then leads me to the stairs and we climb to the second floor.

Papa finds Mom's name on a board hanging outside the room. We enter and see Mom lying on a big bed. I run to her with happiness written all over my face and show her my new black high-heeled shoes.

She simply looks at Papa and says, "Jacob, adjust my headrest so I can sit up."

Papa complies.

"Oh, Jacob, did you know he almost died? When the doctor called the nurse to come and help her, I burst into tears and panicked. I begged her to tell me if my baby was all right. And that's when I saw my little helpless baby, all purple with the umbilical cord around his neck. I screamed and I guess I fainted, because when I opened my eyes, I was in another room with nurses standing over me, assuring me the baby was okay. They told me he will be in intensive care for a while, and no visitors are allowed."

Papa reassured her, "Thank God, it is all over and well."

"Of course, it's easy for you to say since you didn't have to go through what I did. As always, I'm the one dealing with the pain and suffering all by myself."

She goes on and on about my baby brother. I guess she's not interested in my new shoes. I bend down and, with the palm of my hand, shine them. Without really thinking, I leave the room and follow a nurse downstairs. I soon lose track of her, but keep going, not knowing where I'm headed.

I find myself in a room filled with cribs, some holding babies, some empty. I also see a table full of baby bottles. I tiptoe from crib to crib, peeking inside each to see if I can tell which one might be my baby brother. One sign grabs my attention because as I spell it out, it sounds just like my last name, Mikaelian! This must be him!

Why is he hooked to so many tubes? Oh boy, I think I just walked into the intensive care unit! Well, what do they expect? I have to visit my little brother. After all, he is mine to take home and play with. Papa told me so!

Here I stand, surrounded by all the little babies, when I feel a big hand on my shoulder. I turn around and stare at a tall lady dressed all in white, even the hat on top of her head.

In a firm voice, she states, "You must leave this room *right now!*" and she directs me to the door.

I do as she says and return to my mom's room. I have no idea how I find my way back, but I do.

Before my papa and I leave for home, Mom looks at my shoes, then at Papa. "Why did you get her shoes with heels? Take them back and exchange them for a flat pair."

"They aren't so high, Liz."

With a pleading voice, I ask, "Mom, can I please keep them?"

Papa puts his hand on my head, leading me to the door, and says, "Yes, Mom will let you keep your shoes."

As we leave, Mom jealously screeches, "Of course, keep spoiling her!"

I'm excited to get home so I can show off my new black high-heeled shoes to Ed and Eda. *I wonder if they'll like them. I think I just might wear them to bed!*

Homecoming

FOR THE NEXT FEW DAYS, I'm so happy to be spending time with Papa at home since Mom is still in the hospital. He cooks for us, lets us sleep in, and we get to do just about anything we want!

One morning, he leaves me with Ed and Eda and tells us to tidy up the house while he goes to bring Mom and our new baby brother home. As soon as he leaves, we start cleaning the house. I help by straightening up the bedding the best I can. But of course, it is mostly Eda doing the work. At fourteen, she has learned to help around the house and take care of Ed, myself, and, soon, our new baby brother. As she sweeps the rug and dusts, the doorbell rings.

The three of us run to the courtyard, dashing toward the front door. I am now just tall enough to reach the doorknob. Ed unlatches the door so I can open it.

"Hurry up, Ed! Let Mom and Papa come in!" I urge. "I get to hold the baby first!"

Eda pulls the door open. Mom holds a bundle wrapped in a blue baby blanket, and Papa carries Mom's handbag.

I jump up and down so I can see inside the bundle. After what seems like forever, Mom finally sits down on the dining chair and uncovers the baby.

Eda asks, "What's his name?"

"His name is Josh," replies Mom.

Oh, he is so cute! My baby brother has blond hair and light skin like Papa's. He's so white I can see the blue veins under his eyelids!

Upon my first touch, Mom says, "You must be very gentle with him and not hold him if Eda or I are not around." I am so in awe of my new baby brother, I don't really hear what Mom is telling me!

***

Later in the evening, the doorbell rings again. I look at Eda with surprise, as it is unusual to have visitors any time. Mom must have been expecting someone, because she instructs us to go and open the door.

Ed and I race to the courtyard. "Stop pushing me!" I holler at him. "You just want to be first!"

He beats me there and opens the door. In front of us are my four aunties: Janet, Riva, Lydia, and Emma. Behind them stand two big men who are carrying large pieces of furniture. We greet our aunties with hugs and kisses.

Auntie Emma asks, "Is your mom home?"

"Yes, she is! Come see my new baby brother!" I reply with a rush.

Papa, who is making tea in the kitchen, also comes to the door.

"*Barev!*" He greets my aunties and invites them in. I follow them to where Mom and my baby brother are resting. Papa leads the delivery men to the living room to set down the furniture. They bring in a blue crib first, then a wardrobe, followed by a nightstand. Papa reaches in his shirt pocket, gets some money out, and tips the men as they turn to leave.

What is all this stuff? Are they gifts? Who are they for?

Papa believes when there is a group of women, they should be left alone to carry on their private conversations, so he says, "While you ladies are visiting, I'll catch up with my reading." He politely excuses himself, grabs his poetry book by his favorite writer, Hafez, and his pack of cigarettes, and heads back to the kitchen.

I study the furniture, trying to figure out who it belongs to. Tenderly, I run my fingers across the headboard of the wooden crib, which is decorated with a couple of spring chicks, some cracked eggshells, and red, yellow, and white daisies. Ever so carefully, my fingertips trace the paintings. You'd think I was trying to find the smallest imperfection.

As I caress every inch of the headboard, I get closer to the sides made of wooden bars with gaps in between. I try to put my head through the bars, to no avail, but am able to stick my hand through. I even smell the furniture, which must have been painted recently.

After I inspect the crib, it's time to check out the wardrobe. It's a big box on four legs with two doors in front. On each door is also painted yellow spring chicks, shattered eggshells, and colorful daisies, like those of the crib. As I pull the wardrobe doors open, I notice one side of the wardrobe has white shelves and the opposite side has a bar attached to the corners of the inside walls.

I turn to Eda and ask, "What's this bar for?"

"That's where the clothing will be hung," she explains.

My eyes light up, and I run to my mom's room. I have a mission: gather all my clothes and put them in my new wardrobe!

After grabbing my clothes, pillow, and blanket, I press everything to my chest and make my way to the living room. I can hardly see in front of me, but somehow I manage to reach my destination where my family, the crib, and wardrobe are gathered. I have a serious look on my face, knowing I am going to officially claim my new bedroom furniture.

"Girl, what in the world do you think you are doing? That is all clean bedding! Are you crazy?" my mom screams.

I look at her and shiver, thinking she is going to spank me. Lucky for me, she is nursing my baby brother.

Auntie Emma calmly says, "Liz, leave her alone. She's just a bit jealous and curious."

My aunties always try to comfort my mom, in hopes of easing her nerves.

I turn around, drop my clothes on the floor, and commence making my bed the best I can. I am short, so it's hard to put the pillow and blanket in the crib. I stand on my tiptoes and stretch over the crib. Once I am done, I pick up my clothes from the floor and walk toward the wardrobe. I open the door and squeeze everything inside and shut it. Then I turn around and stand in front of it, with a sense of being watched.

"Feel better now?" Mom asks.

I don't know what to say. I'm happy to have completed my mission, but I'm scared also. Suddenly, Josh burps, taking the attention away from me. I look at him and put my hand over my mouth, expecting Mom to get mad, but she does just the opposite! She and my aunties grin and chime together, "Good boy!"

I'm confused. Mom has always said it's rude to burp. Now my baby brother does it and gets praised?

All I care about is getting into my bed and enjoying it. I wait for my Aunties Janet, Emma, Riva, and Lydia to leave, then decide to go try it out.

I get closer to the railings, hold on to the top one, and pull myself up. *Now what?*

As I'm standing on the edge of the bar, Ed comes closer to me and says, "*Esh*, bend your head down."

As I do, I feel his hands on my butt as he pushes me into the crib head first. Ed had his fun. My nose hurts a little, but I couldn't care less. *Hooray! I'm in my new bed!*

I try to lie down, but the bed is a bit small for me. I can't stretch my legs! Oh well. I bend my knees, pull the blanket over me, and fall asleep.

***

The next morning, I wake up to Papa's whistling. I sit up in my bed with Eda on one side and Ed on the other. I'm confused. *How come I'm not in my crib? I know I fell asleep there!*

"What happened to my crib?" I ask Papa.

He calmly replies, "The crib is for little babies. You are my big girl. That's why I'm going to take you with me to buy some fresh bread."

Still sad but instantly interested, I ask, "Just you and me, Papa?"

"Of course, *Baless*. Just you and me."

Bridge

I HURRY OFF to the dining room to change from my nightgown into my house clothes.

"It's a little windy. Be sure to put warm clothes on, *Baless*," Papa suggests.

Eda walks in to help me change and brush my hair. We always get dressed in the dining room, as I've been taught that no one should see our body when we change, not even our father or brother.

"Okay, Eda, I'm ready!" I am so excited about going with Papa.

"Wait, Ariana. Let me finish fixing your hair." Eda twists a rubber band around my ponytail.

"Can I go now?"

"Oh, gosh! You can't wait, can you?" I keep moving away from her as she tries to make sure my sweater is buttoned up. "All right, now you can go."

By now, Papa stands in the courtyard, singing and looking around. From behind me, Eda calls, "Your shoes, Ariana!"

I'm in such a rush I forgot to put my shoes on! I turn around, grab my black high-heeled shoes from the side of the balcony, sit down, and put them on. Placing my little palms on the cold, red-bricked floor, I push myself up and turn around to make sure I haven't messed up the order of the other shoes in the lineup along the wall. That is a big no-no.

After straightening them up, I take a few steps to the edge of the balcony and jump. Jumping off the balcony is something Ed and I always do together. He's the one who teaches me crazy things. It's so much fun and makes me giggle. Sometimes Mom lets us play and jump off the balcony, but other times, she gets mad at us.

I know Papa is there to catch me. After he gently puts me down, we walk hand in hand toward the entry door.

The wind is blowing, the clouds are forming, and the air smells fresh. "Oh, it makes me feel so good to breathe this clean air, Ariana. Try it, *Shoonig*," he encourages. This is Papa's nickname for me, since I am like his little puppy.

I do. "Oh, it does feel good, Papa!" It's been a long time since I have been this happy.

We come upon the entry door under the big oak tree. On one side is an old wooden door and behind it is a toilet. Most of the older houses have their toilet built in the backyard in a small cabin, and it's the kind where you must squat over it. But Hamlet's toilet is indoors, and you can actually sit on it. Papa calls it an "American-style" toilet. On the other side of the entry door, the broken bicycle leans against the wall. It seems a day does not pass when I don't ask Mom, Papa, Ed, or Eda why I can't ride this bicycle. The answer is always the same, short and not so sweet, "It is broken."

I can't stop looking at the red bicycle and touching the flat tire. Glancing back at my papa, I notice he's smiling at me. "You little monster. You know what's wrong with it, don't you?"

"Yes, Papa. It needs air like Hamlet's bicycle. You can fix it, right?" I ask excitedly.

"I will try Ariana," he says. But I think in his heart, he knows he's not able to fix the broken tire and doesn't want to disappoint me.

We walk toward the unpaved sidewalk. Still holding Papa's big strong hand, I start swinging my arm back and forth. At the same time, I begin to skip. Every time I do, my braided hair swings side to side like a pendulum. The faster I skip, the faster my braid bounces. Sometimes my hair hits my face. Elated, I just keep going.

As I skip along the riverside, I decide to show Papa I can throw a rock across the river just like Ed.

I let go of his hand, bend over, and pick up a piece of rock. I move it between my little fingers to make sure I have the correct grip. Then, twisting my hip, I bring my arm back, and with one quick turn, let go.

Together we watch the rock sail to the other side of the river, waiting to hear the rock hit another rock. In a split second, we hear the clank of contact, then the following echo.

"Did you hear that, Papa?"

He looks at me so proudly. "Yes, I heard it! That was amazing, *Shoonig*! Who taught you to throw a rock like that?"

"Ed taught me, Papa!" I announce with pride, holding my head up. "Papa, you have to see how far Ed can throw a rock!"

"He must be very good, because he taught you very well. Maybe one day, you can teach your little brother how to throw rocks."

I become quiet as I start thinking about Josh, but that doesn't stop me from skipping and kicking the pebbles of the unpaved sidewalk. Papa is whistling and pauses now and then to say hello in the Persian manner to a neighbor. He gently puts his hand on his chest, bends his head forward a bit, and says, "*Salam*." And if the neighbor is female, Papa completely avoids any eye contact. It is the polite, religious way of respecting women in Iran.

We have a little ways to go before we get to the alley on the right side of the sidewalk. To the left is a big, long bridge, the only connection between the two neighborhoods.

The bridge is cement with double metal railings on each side. These railings are painted green, but in some areas, the metal is exposed.

Papa told me once that originally the bridge was wooden and one day, when the river flooded, it was washed away. The new, strong concrete bridge was built to replace the old one, and it would never collapse.

As Papa and I approach the bridge, he meets one of his old friends and they start visiting. Standing next to Papa, I gently brush hair from my face that the spring breeze has blown into my eyes.

Spotting the bridge, I slip away and rush toward it. I have learned a trick from Ed, and I just have to show my papa!

I hear him call after me, "Ariana, stop running!"

I am too excited to obey, so I continue my mad dash to the railing. Placing my tiny little hands on the top, I put one foot on the bottom. With a jerk, I pull up my other foot, standing up straight and tall.

"Ariana, hold onto the rail!" Papa wails.

This is the moment I let go, waving both my hands in the air. I can't understand why he is panicking and asking me to hold on. This is the best part of the trick!

It doesn't take long for him to reach me. He holds me tight and pulls me back down onto the bridge. Gripping my hands, with a firm voice he says, "Don't ever do that again, Ariana!"

I am confused and sad at the same time. *Why is Papa so upset?* I begin to cry.

Realizing what he's done, he puts his hand on my head and hugs me, something he hardly ever does.

"You scared me, Ariana. You could have fallen down and gotten hurt, *Baless*."

Even though I don't really comprehend what he's telling me, I shake my head and promise, "I'll never do it again, Papa, never."

He takes my hand and leads me from the bridge. A few paces later, Papa swings me up and onto his shoulders. With his big, strong hands securely around my dangling ankles, I feel safe.

The Breadman
and His Helper

PAPA AND I ENTER the narrow alley, where the canal runs down its center. Sadly, some citizens carelessly dump their trash in the canal, causing the water to back up and create an awful smell. The residents who live in the houses on either side of the alley complain about the odor, yet they continue to do it.

"What is the canal for?" I ask Papa, as I have a hundred times before.

Patiently he tells me yet again, just as if it is the first time, "The canal is made to direct the rain water to the big sewage system so the streets won't flood."

I hold my nose real tight and breathe through my mouth. Still sitting on Papa's strong shoulders, with my other hand, I mess with his thinning, dark brown hair.

As we pass through the alley, Papa starts to sing a silly song, and of course I sing along, still holding my nose:

> *Mom will ride by carriage*
> *Sister will ride by buggy*
> *Dad will ride by a lame donkey*
> *He always gets the blame.*
> *Mom gets the fur coat*
> *Sister gets the heavy coat*
> *Dad gets the buttonless, torn shirt*
> *He always gets the blame.*

We giggle together and Papa says, "*Shoonig*, you know you have a beautiful voice."

This makes me laugh so hard, it brings tears to my eyes. I know exactly what he's talking about. When I sing, it comes out squeaky and funny.

As Papa chuckles, I continue singing with my funny voice and feel carefree. He gently taps on my foot and says, "Okay, little girl, the ride is over. We have arrived."

"Are we there already, Papa?"

"Yes, we are." He points to the bakery, lifts me up over his head by my waist, and puts me down. As he holds my hand, we both walk inside.

The bakery is long and narrow with chalky walls and a concrete floor covered with pebbles and gravel. A big brick oven stands in the middle of the store, where the bread is baked twice a day.

Standing beside the brick oven, feeling the heat from the fire in its bottom, I can't wait to see the baker make the bread!

The baker is a tall young man with dark, short, curly hair, a thick moustache, and a big nose. Standing behind a long wooden table, he grabs a ball of dough with one hand and sprinkles white flour on the table with his other. Throwing the dough on the table, he presses down on it with the tips of his fingers, making it nice and flat. Next, using the rolling pin, he rolls it back and forth over the dough until it's shaped like a long rectangle. He takes a big wooden paddle covered with a white sheet of cloth and sprays some water on it. Carefully transferring the dough to the paddle, the baker takes a few steps toward the hot brick oven and with one quick move, slides the dough inside. He's very good at his job, and yet I wonder how many times he has burned his hands.

After a few minutes, the baker goes back to the table for a long metal fork and approaches the oven. In a flash, he sticks the fork inside, stabs the bread, and tosses the fresh loaf of heaven onto the table. Oh, it smells so good! I can't wait to eat a slice!

I reach for the bread, but Papa says, "Wait up, *Baless*. The bread is too hot and it can burn your hand."

I have to wait ever so patiently while Papa buys *several* loaves.

On our way home, it starts to drizzle. Papa tries to make me walk faster by pulling my hand and taking bigger, faster steps. I'm almost running now, trying to keep up. He's singing another one of his silly songs. What fun! Hand in hand, me and my papa.

We soon arrive home, and Papa rings the bell. Waiting, we smile at one another, droplets of water dripping off the tips of our noses, as it begins to pour and the thunder echoes.

Papa exclaims, "We made it home just in time!"

Behind the door we hear Ed's voice, loudly asking, "Who is it?"

Papa replies, "The bread man and his helper! Open up, young man."

Ed swings the door open and we quickly enter the front yard. By now, the rain is coming down in sheets, so we all run up the stairs toward the balcony of our house.

"Take off your shoes and put them aside, so your mother will not get angry," Papa instructs me.

I look at him and nod. Taking my time, I put my black high-heeled shoes against the wall, turn, and stand on my tiptoes to reach for the door handle. I hear Ed's voice behind me. "Hurry up!" Before he can finish his command, we are already moving inside.

I notice Eda has picked up our bedding, wrapped it neatly, and placed it in one corner of the room, creating space for our breakfast time. On days when Papa is not home, we eat breakfast in the dark kitchen on the little wooden table. But when he is, we have our meals on a hand-woven Persian rug on the dining room floor. I don't like sitting on this itchy rug. It's so rough and almost always scratches my knees or elbows. All I can do to make it feel better is to rub them with my spit. I've seen Ed do this for his scraped knees, too.

Eda lays down a square cotton tablecloth in the middle of the rug as Mom brings in a big tray with plates, teacups, bread, butter, and a jar of her homemade fig jam. Eda fetches the serving dish full of omelets and we all sit down, ready for our breakfast. Josh is sleeping in his crib.

Papa goes first. He gets a big piece of bread and carefully holds it in the palm of his hand. With a large spoon in his other hand, he scoops a big helping of the omelet with tomatoes on it, securely rolls the bread, and passes a sandwich to each of us. Of course, it's me who gets the very first one.

"*Anoosh!*" Papa says.

I'm so hungry! I enjoy my sandwich in my favorite sitting place, right next to Papa, while the storm outside rages.

"Liz, please eat your sandwich. Since you are nursing the baby, you need to keep up your strength," Papa says.

"But I'm not hungry," Mom replies coldly. But Papa insists, so she accepts the sandwich and begins to eat.

We're almost done with our breakfast when Mom tells Eda to start washing the dishes. I like helping Eda, so I pick up the leftover pieces of bread and the jar of fig jam and go to the balcony. I pause to watch the storm, then scurry to the kitchen as the lightning strikes.

Eda grabs the bread and the jar of jam from me, puts them in their place, and says, "Go get the rest and be careful not to drop anything. Be quick so we can spend more time with Papa!"

"Oh, I will, Eda!"

I skip back to the living room, where Mom is putting the teacups we've just used on a big tray. I decide I won't even *try* to pick up that tray. I might drop it and break everything.

While I'm lost in my own thoughts, Mom commands, "What are you waiting for? Hurry and take this tray to Eda!"

I am afraid of what might happen but do it anyway. "Yes, Mom. Eda said if I hurry and help her clean up quickly, we can spend more time with Papa."

Mom looks at me with a frown. "Of course, she *would* say that. The only time you help me out is when your father is home. You spoiled worthless kids!"

Mom's angry words sting but don't deter me from finishing the task quickly.

At last, the living room is all clean and tidy. Ed, Eda, and I sit with Papa in the living room. Soon, I start to tumble on the scratchy rug and Ed joins in. I'm so happy! Often Ed and I tumble and play "Horsey" with each other, but not Eda. She just sits in a corner and watches.

Every time we tumble, Papa claps for us, which makes me do it even more. He says, "When you tumble, as soon as you roll, raise your hands and pull yourself up. That will help you stand up just like a Russian gymnast."

I roll just like he says.

"What a fast learner you are, *Shoonig*. You could be a good gymnast one day! I'm going to sign you up for classes as soon as I can."

I don't know what a "gymnast" is, but I think I'd like to be one, just for him.

Four More Days

ED AND EDA ARE DOING their homework, but I already finished mine earlier. Mom sits on the colorful, rough rug in the corner of our dining room, knitting next to the kerosene heater, and Josh naps next to her. A yellow tea kettle sits on the heater, steam rising from its short spout.

Her hands move quickly with the thick purple yarn wrapped around her fingers, the knitting needles in her hands—tips of silver metal touching each other—clicking with each move as the bundle of yarn skitters around on the floor. Periodically, she stops, moves the rows on the needles, looks at the loops, then continues knitting. Sometimes, when Ed, Eda, or I ask her a question, she won't answer, only moans, "Wait, I'm counting my loops." We know better than to disturb her.

Often, she asks me to help her make a ball out of the yarn bundle, as she did earlier today. I sat down and held my arms straight out. Separating it from the center, she put it around my arms. Holding the ends of the yarn between her two fingers, she began wrapping it around and around, until a ball formed. She continued the wrapping until there was none left around my arms. She did this really fast, but my arms got so tired, I began to drop them.

Firmly she scolded, "Hold your hands up, Ariana. Don't move."

Sometimes there's a knot or two in the yarn and Mom must stop and carefully undo them. I don't like it when that happens. It makes my arms ache. Today, thank goodness, there were no knots.

When Mom is knitting and Ed and Eda are doing homework, the house is really quiet, so quiet I can hear myself breathing. The only noise in the room is the clicking of the knitting needles.

I get up and go to the window, where I can better hear the wind whistling outside. It tosses the leaves in the air, twirling and twisting, just like when Eda holds both my hands in hers and turns me around really fast. I especially love it when she stops and lets go. My head spins and I collapse, laughing hysterically. I chase the leaves with my eyes as they float up in the air and fall back to the ground, often to just get picked up again and fly away to another corner of the yard or float back to the tops of the trees.

I don't see many birds outside at all. Papa told me once that when it's cold, all the birds migrate to a warmer place, far from our home. I think that's where they must be now. Instead, I see a stray cat making his way quietly, slowly, on the ledge of the tall brick wall. It's the same gray and white cat I often see passing by our house. This cat had stolen a baby bird once, and Ed decided to teach him a lesson with his slingshot!

The sky gets darker, and it begins to rain. Then I notice Miss Mary with a maroon knit wrap around her shoulders, standing on her balcony, holding a black umbrella. As she comes down the stairs, the wind blows her umbrella from side to side as she tries hard not to let go.

"Mom! Mom! Miss Mary's coming!" I announce.

"Okay! What great news! I wonder what she wants."

We hardly ever have visitors. But when we do, Ed, Eda, and I love it! It breaks the silence in our house.

Right before Miss Mary climbs up our stairs, Mom tells us, "Behave and don't embarrass me!"

Ed runs to open the door, then hurries back to his seat to continue doing his homework. I stand by the door, and the cold air knifes through to my bones as she enters.

Mom puts away her knitting to greet her.

Miss Mary is a very nice, educated lady, and the principal of an Armenian school where her son, Hamlet goes. Her husband, Mr. Arman, teaches English there. Mom and Papa always say they are the nicest landlords anyone could have.

"Please take a seat here near the table, Mary," Mom invites. Miss Mary never sits on the floor, even if she were to crochet or read a book. She's used to sitting on her nice couch, something we don't own.

As she goes to sit down, she gently hugs me and asks, "How are you, Miss Ariana?"

"I'm just fine, Miss Mary."

Then she turns to Ed and Eda. "Good kids. Study hard!"

Mom interrupts and asks her, "Would you like a cup of tea?"

"No, thank you, Liz. I must get back. I'm preparing dinner. I came to invite you and your kids to Hamlet's sixth birthday."

"Oh, my goodness! He's six already? Well, when is it?"

I keep looking from Miss Mary to Mom while they carry on their conversation. I'm so excited! This means I'll get to go to Hamlet's house and play with his toys!

"Other guests will arrive at one o'clock Sunday afternoon," answers Miss Mary. "We'll have lunch and cake."

"Thank you for your invitation. We'll be there."

Miss Mary gets up, places her wrap back around her shoulders, and says to me, "You'll get to meet Hamlet's new friends from his school."

I wonder how many new friends he has and what games will we play? I remember his last birthday party when Mr. Arman made a big maze on their dining room floor out of colorful crayons. All of us kids had to walk between the twisted lines without touching them. The winner received a delicious chocolate-covered cupcake. Then we played musical chairs, and whoever was the last one sitting got an extra scoop of homemade vanilla ice cream. But the best fun was when Hamlet sat on the floor with his brightly wrapped presents surrounding him. I always get to sit close to him, so I get a good look at his new toys. That is so cool!

My thoughts are interrupted when Miss Mary walks out the door, grabs her umbrella, and quickly leaves our balcony. As the strong wind blows, Mom shuts the door behind her and gets back to her knitting.

"Mom, how many days is it till Hamlet's birthday?"

"There are many days! You better stop asking before you drive me crazy! When it's time to go, I'll let you know!"

I approach the table where Eda is doing her homework quietly. I sit on the floor near her feet, gently grab the corner of her skirt, and pull it. Eda peers from the corners of her eyes; a wordless look with upturned hands, *What?*

I try to whisper, but I'm still loud, "How many more days to Hamlet's birthday?"

Eda shows me four fingers, then puts one finger to her lips to silence me.

I pull myself to get back up and ease toward the window. The clouds have subdued all light. The wind rattles everything that's loose and rain comes down in torrents. On the left side of our balcony, I see the lights from Hamlet's dining room. I count my fingers to four. Eda explained, every time it gets dark and we go to sleep, it's one day. So that means four more sleeps! Oh, I am disappointed. It just seems so far away!

I imagine Miss Mary getting things ready for Hamlet's birthday party in their dining room and wonder if he's the only kid who has birthday parties.

Summer Surprise

TONIGHT, AS WE EAT SUPPER on our balcony, Ed, Eda, and I hear someone whistling in the distance. I jump up and run to the door calling, "Papa! Papa's home!" We can always recognize his whistling just as we can his footsteps.

Ed is right behind me and opens the door. "Papa!" I yell and jump into his arms.

"Barev, Shoonig!" Papa holds me close and rustles Ed's hair. Eda approaches, too, as does Mom. Papa pats Eda's shoulder and greets Mom with a "hello."

Papa then reaches inside his pants pocket and pulls out a stack of money. Before we know it, money is showering about us! The three of us lean down to collect as much as we can.

Mom smirks and remarks, "Better be more than you brought home last time."

***

Papa reads the afternoon newspaper, something he always does when he's home. He can sit somewhere and read for hours! Mom hand-washes some clothes in a wash bucket, since we still don't have a washing machine. Josh plays with his toys next to Mom.

I sit on the stairs trying to chase little road ants with a twig, another Ed-taught trick! Sometimes I just hold it in front of the ants and watch them detour around and around themselves, as they try to find their way.

Mom asks Papa, "Does it ever occur to you to maybe take us somewhere for a vacation before I die? Everyone I know goes somewhere at least for a week, except us. Do you even think about my life? All day, every day, I wash, cook, and clean for these kids!"

"What do you want me to do, Liz? Where can I take you? I don't have a car."

"Can't you borrow Miktar's car and take us to the beach for once? These kids have no idea what one looks like. Your brother has taken his family many times already. Can't I have a little fun in my life?"

In a raised voice, which only happens when Papa's upset, he states, "I am not going to ask my brother to give me his transportation so I can take you on vacation."

"Why not, Jacob?"

I jump in and ask, "How *does* the beach look anyway, Papa?"

He puts his newspaper down and looks at me with his head cocked to one side. "You really don't know?"

"No, Papa. I've never seen one. I think I saw a picture of cousin Nina at the beach last summer, but I don't really know how big it is."

Papa pauses for a minute and looks at Mom. "I'll see what I can do. Maybe I'll be able to borrow Miktar's car. But how will we pay for everything?"

"I've saved up some money. Plus, I'll cook all our meals. We'll just need money to pay for the hut, and we can stay in a cheaper area."

Papa shrugs and tilts his head in agreement! I run to him. "So, we're going? We're going?" I jump up and down, and then run to the dining room where Ed and Eda are playing a homemade board game.

"Ed, Eda, we're going to the beach!" I announce.

They both look at me like I'm crazy.

"Says who?" asks Ed.

"Papa! He told me just now!" I grab his hand and pull him to come with me. "If you don't believe me, ask him yourself."

With Ed and me in the yard, and Eda standing on the balcony now, I address Papa, "Tell them you are going to take us to the beach, Papa."

Ed and Eda hold their breath in anticipation.

Papa calmly replies, "I will try. I don't know for sure yet. Let me go talk to your uncle tomorrow and then I will decide."

I'm so excited, I want to announce it to the whole world!

Mom douses our excitement. "All right, calm down. Don't get your hopes up. Knowing your father, he most likely will go see your uncle tomorrow, but he'll *never* ask for his car."

I try not to lose hope, but Eda has been disappointed so many times, she just heads back to the game.

Ignoring Mom's comment, Papa says, "Am I the only one who's hungry? Can we eat something?"

"If I ever finish washing and hanging these clothes to dry, we will!" Mom snaps.

"I have an idea, Liz," Papa says. "I can ask my friend at the garage, Ali, if his wife can come and help you whenever you need her. She is a housekeeper."

"Ask her. But can you pay her?"

"Don't worry. God willing, I will get more jobs. Also, I can pay for the hut because one of my friends owes me money."

"Of course. You're always giving our money away."

Papa forces a grin and turns to Eda. "My daughter, since your mother is busy, can you set the table?"

I grab the bread and Eda gets the pot of beef cutlets Mom made earlier. We bring our supper to the balcony, Papa lays the tablecloth on the floor, and we all sit down to eat.

Thoughts of the beach swim in my head. Even when I go to bed, I pray we get to go.

Papa leaves the next morning to see my uncle. He's gone all day. We are all eager to find out what's going to happen!

When the sun is almost gone, Papa finally comes home. I run to him and he tosses me up in the air. "Papa, Papa, are you going to take us? Did you talk to Uncle? Is he going to let you have his car?"

"Hold on, *Baless*. I'll let you know in a minute."

Papa and I approach the balcony where Ed and Eda are waiting for his answer. He looks at the three of us, unable to hold back the grin spreading across his face. "Yes, we will go."

I cover my mouth with both hands. I can't believe what I just heard! Even Mom still doesn't know. She's in her bedroom putting Josh to sleep. Ed, Eda, and I barrage Papa with all kinds of questions.

He finally answers, "In a few days, we will pack and go to the beach for a week, but you have to promise me something. Don't bother your mom with questions about the trip. It's best not to talk about it."

The three of us zip our lips and toss away the keys in promise.

The Magnificent Sunrise

FINALLY, THE DAY HAS ARRIVED! Early in the morning, Papa returns with my uncle's car. He parks by the main street since the path to our house is too narrow for a car. It takes Papa, Ed, and Eda several trips to get all our luggage in the car.

When the car is packed, Papa claps once and says, "All aboard! Time to go!"

As Ed and I cheer, Mom asks, "How long will it take us to get there, Jacob?"

"About seven hours, but we're going to make it fun. I'll stop a couple of times so you and the kids can stretch."

I really don't comprehend how long seven hours is, but it really doesn't matter to me.

We all pile in. Mom sits in the front, holding Josh in her lap. Ed and Eda each get a window seat with me in the middle. Papa starts the car.

Here we go! Yay! I giggle and slide my bottom to the edge of the leather seat. I place one hand on the side of Mom's seat and the other on Papa's.

"Papa, how far is the seaside?"

"It's pretty far."

"Papa, how many days can we swim?"

With joy in his voice, he says, "For seven days."

"That's great, Papa!"

"Hush up," Mom says harshly and starts talking to Papa.

I don't even hear what she says as I wiggle in my seat and accidentally touch Ed's leg.

"Move, you *esh*!" Ed complains.

"But I want to be close to the window, too!"

Ed elbows me and I try not to cry. "You hurt me, Ed!"

"Oh shut up, both of you!" Mom screams, turning halfway in her seat and slapping me on my leg.

I can't help it. Disappointed, I scoot back. With the palms of my hands, I wipe my face. Eda gently rubs her hand on my thigh and wraps her arm around me. Veering cars and big trucks honking around us distracts my mood.

"Papa, are we at the seaside already?" I ask, only a few minutes later.

Papa laughs. "No, *Baless*. We are just getting close to Karaj. Soon, we will stop near the dam, so you can see the water it holds."

"How much longer, Papa?"

"Can you just *shut up* for a minute?" Mom yells.

"Liz, don't get mad at her, please. She's just an excited little girl."

"Here we go again. You just have to defend that brat of yours."

Before long, Papa stops and tells us to get out but to stay really close to him. "We're near the largest dam in the country," he says, moving closer to the edge. "It's called Karaj. This was built by the order of Reza Shah Kabir, the Shah's father."

"Keep the kids away, Jacob!" Mom commands as she holds Josh tightly to her chest.

The wind blows cool mist onto my face, and the sound of roaring water is so loud I can't hear half the things Papa says. He stands behind me, his hands on my shoulders, with Ed and Eda beside him.

Our next stop is the city of Rasht. "This is one of the largest cities in the northern part of Iran," Papa tells us.

I know he's trying to give us as much information as he can, but all I care about is getting to the beach!

Early in the afternoon, we arrive at our destination. I sit sideways, really close to Eda, with my nose pressed to the window.

White sand is everywhere with lots of young boys standing around. As we pass by, they mumble at us.

"Papa, what are they saying?" I ask.

"They're announcing they have huts for rent." He slows down near one of the boys and asks the price for a hut. Once they've agreed, the local boy gives Papa directions to ours.

As soon as we get there, another boy shows us the place where we'll be staying. Ed and I can't wait, whereas Eda doesn't look too excited.

As Papa starts moving our luggage to the hut, Ed and I run to the beach as fast as we can. Of course, Ed is much faster, so I scream, "Ed, wait up! Wait for me!"

I run on the warm sand, following Ed all the way to the sea. I stop abruptly as a big wave rushes to my toes. My feet sink in the sand and my body rocks back. Trying to keep my balance, I notice the seashells and tiny fish in the sand.

Some people swim; others play ball or build sand castles.

Ooh, the water feels good! I try to absorb it all.

Ed comes closer and sticks his hand in the sand, grabs a large seashell, and puts it to his ear.

"What is it, Ed?"

"Be quiet." He listens some more.

"I wanna listen, too!"

"Go get your own. This is mine."

"Please, Ed? I don't know where to find one."

"Here, whiny baby." He puts the seashell to my ear and I listen closely for what Ed had heard, but I can't hear anything.

"Ed, let's go back and ask Mom if we can change and swim. I can't wait any longer!" It's hard to run on sand. My feet get stuck, and the sand is burning them, making me run even harder!

Ed and I make it to our hut. Breathing heavily, I ask, "Mom, can I go swimming, please?"

"No, you can't. You should wait for your father. Since you don't know how to swim, you have to be with him."

Anxiously, I look around to see where Papa is. "Mom, where is Papa?"

"I don't know." Mom sounds upset. "I'm sure 'Chatterbox' has found a friend and is talking instead of helping me organize this room or spending time with me." She's almost talking to herself, and I am unsure of what will happen next. Grazing along the straw of the hut's wall, I slowly distance myself from Mom and sit near Ed and Eda on the stairs. I hope Papa comes back soon before Mom gets too upset.

I see a few men having a conversation off near the cabana where someone is grilling corn. *There he is!* "Papa!"

He turns around, and I run to him with all my might. "Can we go swimming, Papa?"

"Quiet, I am talking," Papa scolds. I can't help but feel disappointed. I want Papa to come with me and take me swimming. I turn around and go back to the hut.

Mom has made us baloney sandwiches, and we start eating without Papa. Afterwards, Mom takes Josh and tells us to put on our bathing suits; that she is going to take us to the sea. "But you have to stay near me," Mom says.

Ed, Eda, and I look at each other, amazed *she* is going to take us swimming!

The borrowed bathing suit I begin to change into wasn't really made for swimming. A one-piece pink ballet costume with little orange ruffles around the waist, it was given to me by an old Russian lady who used to live in our neighborhood. Of course, it makes no difference to me, even if it does look odd.

At last, I'm ready to go to the water, as are Ed and Eda. With Mom in front of us, I jump down into the sand. I hear Papa. "Liz? Liz, I'll be there soon!" Mom ignores him and keeps walking.

We stand at the edge where the water washes over my feet. Ed and Eda walk in up to their knees. Mom, Josh, and I sit on the shore where the waves end.

Soon enough, Papa joins us. He puts me on his shoulders, takes me further out, and throws me into a wave. I go under, and up he scoops me. I get the taste of the salty water in my mouth. Yuck!

Ed tries to swim, and Papa encourages him. "Kick, kick, and move your arms!"

Eda joins in, and we all have the best time. The sunny day is warm and the water feels so good.

Papa says to me, "Why don't you stay with Josh so I can take your mother for a swim?"

"I can play with Josh, Papa. I'll watch you from there!"

"Good girl."

I sit with Josh, making sand castles with my baby brother as Papa holds Mom's hand, taking her farther into the water. Eda comes to help me take care of Josh.

For the next few days, we do more of the same. We are loving it! Sometimes Mom goes to play Bingo with a group of people. And she's only gotten mad at us a few times!

Tonight, during dinner, Papa tells Mom, "Before we leave, I'm going to take Ariana to see the sunrise."

Ed questions, "Are we going home, Papa?"

"Of course, we can't stay here forever, but we can come back another time," Papa reassures.

"Really, Papa? Will you bring us back?"

Mom mockingly says, "Sure you will. And God only knows when that'll happen."

I refuse to let Mom ruin his surprise and ask, "Papa, where are you going to take me?"

"To see the sunrise, *Baless*. I'll wake you up very early in the morning."

"Leave it alone, Jacob. Are you kidding me? You are going to wake her up to see the sunrise? You are out of your mind."

Papa smiles at Mom and says, "It's worth it. She will always remember it."

"I can't wait, Papa. I will go with you."

Night soon comes and we all lie down. I try to imagine the sun in the morning, and I fall asleep.

***

A whisper in my ear says, "Ariana, wake up." I open my eyes to see Papa smiling at me. He holds my hand and directs me to the door. He grabs a blanket and wraps it around me, puts on his shirt, and off we go!

It's still dark outside, but the lights around the huts lead our way to the beach. The sea breeze is cold on my skin. Even with the blanket wrapped around me, I shiver. The sand is cool to my feet, so different from the daytime.

Amidst the crashing of the waves, Papa tells me, "What you are about to see, *Baless*, is going to stay in your mind for the rest of your life. You will never forget it."

I try to process what he is saying. With my pajama pants rolled up, I can tell we are standing near the water since the sand feels wetter and the waves touch my feet.

With my hand in his, Papa lifts our arms, pointing to the end of the sea. "Ariana, look!"

The sea becomes calm and relaxed. "Papa, what happened to all the waves?" I hardly finish my question before I see this giant golden ball come out of the water at the end of the sea.

"You see, Ariana? See the majesty in God's work?"

Then he is silent, as am I. This ball keeps rising slowly, and the higher it gets, the brighter it becomes. It looks more like a huge golden cup, and before long, it is the ginormous sun standing in the sky.

What I see is nothing close to what I imagined. Papa was right, I am never, ever going to forget this. Somehow, with Papa, everything is magical, even the sunrise.

That Smile

IN JUST A FEW MORE MONTHS, I'll be done with third grade! Alas, this means Ed will be going to high school, calling me an "elementary baby."

This morning before we leave for school, Mom tells us, "I'm going to visit your grandparents today. I'll be taking Josh with me, so when you get home, you'll be on your own. Make some cheese sandwiches and do your homework. I'll be back before dark."

All day long in class, I think about how much fun it's gonna be without Mom at home. When I get there, Ed and Eda are already waiting for me because Miss Mary had insisted Mom and Papa send me to Catholic school where I can learn more Armenian. My school has lots of mean nuns, and I don't like them one bit. Plus, I go to school by bus and I come home later than Ed and Eda.

Eda tells me to wash my hands and change into my house clothes. As I do, she brings us a tray with slices of pound cake. Ed and I sit on the floor while Eda passes us our plates.

"Be careful not to drop any crumbs, Ariana," Eda warns, then turns to Ed. "You, too. You're worse than Ariana!"

"Oh, Eda. Stop being Mom," says Ed carelessly.

"Shut up, Ed."

All is quiet until Ed's eyes light up and a naughty smile grows on his face. Taking a bite of my yummy cake, I know the wheels are turning in his head.

"What are you cooking up?" Eda asks Ed. "I know you're up to no good."

"Ha, you know we can watch TV before Mom comes home."

"No, we can't. The TV is locked and Mom has the key," Eda says.

"Well, I can fix that. Watch and learn," Ed replies with a butter knife in his hand.

I'm excited to see what Ed has up his sleeve. He sits in front of our brand new black-and-white television set. A big, black, shiny cabinet holds it inside, but a lock keeps it hidden. Only Mom has the key.

"What do you think you're doing?" Eda asks.

"Wait up. You'll see," and Ed begins to squeeze the knife between the crack in the doors.

"Ed, you'll break the lock or scratch the door! Mom will kill you! Stop it!"

But Ed sticks with his plan. With one push, *pop*, the doors unlock. Ed cheers, but I'm worried.

Eda moves closer to the TV and starts examining the doors. "Ah, *esh*!" She smacks Ed in the head. "Look what you did! You scratched the door! You idiot! You're dead meat when Mom comes home!"

Ed shrugs and says, "She won't see it. It's so tiny."

He turns the TV on, and the three of us sit closely like statues, glued to the screen. Our mischief fills us with worry, but we try to enjoy the moment. A comedy show comes on, and Eda says, "It's Charlie Chaplin!"

Our black-and-white TV shows a skinny man with a funny moustache, black hat, and cane. He doesn't talk, but his acting makes us drown in laughter.

***

Time passes too quickly. Eda nearly comes out of her skin when she hears Mom opening the door to the yard. Ed jumps up, turns the TV off, closes the double doors, and hurriedly sits down to open his books. I open my notebook and pretend to write my homework. Eda tries to find a page in her book.

Mom walks in.

"Hi, Mom," we all greet her in unison.

Josh is asleep in Mom's arms. "Let me put the baby down. I'll come back to check on you." Mom leaves for her bedroom.

Knowing none of us has done any of our homework, panic fills us.

Soon she returns. "Let me see your homework," she orders me. Looking at the blank page in my notebook, she grabs my ear and pulls it hard. "What have you been doing while I was gone?"

I'm in pain, but I'm even more scared. I know she's about to find out.

Turning to Ed, she yanks his notebook, yelling, "What the heck have you been doing? Not your schoolwork! Horse playing?"

As she rants, she moves toward the TV and places her hand on the cabinet. She feels the warmth. Fury fills her face as she focuses on Ed. "You little bastard!" She lunges at Ed and begins her merciless attack.

Eda runs to me, pulling me aside.

Mom screams at the top of her lungs, slapping Ed over and over. Hunkered down, Ed begs, "Please don't hit me. I am so sorry. Please, Mom. I won't do it again!"

Ed's pleas only seem to feed Mom's rage as she begins kicking him on the floor. "You monster! Worthless bastard! I wish you were dead! I hope you burn in hell!" Mom rants.

I choke on my tears, holding onto my sister. *Oh, poor Ed.* His face is all red and full of fear.

Just when I think she's done, Mom picks up the dining room chair and throws it at Ed. It breaks as it hits him.

Taking shallow breaths and holding onto his hurt arm, Ed sobs.

Eda and I beg for Ed's life as we hug one another.

Mom stops for just a second, still cursing at Ed, then leaves.

Eda tries to calm him down by holding his shoulders and cleaning his face. I crouch in the corner of the room.

"Eda, where did she go?" I ask.

"I don't know. I wish . . . I wish she'd never come back," Ed stutters. "I hate her!"

I rub my wet eyes with my shirt. "If Papa was home, this never would have happened."

We try to comfort each other during Mom's absence. After about an hour, she shows up with my strong Uncle Ted.

"How did he get here?" I whisper to Eda.

"I don't know, but he looks angry."

Uncle Ted steps away from Mom and storms toward Ed. His hand whacks Ed's face, knocking him to the ground.

"You worthless son-of-a-bitch! You are a shame to this family! You dare to talk back to your mother? And destroy the house?"

He picks up a broken piece of the solid wood chair and hits Ed across his back and feet.

Eda and I both scream. "Stop it, Uncle Ted! Please! He didn't break the chair!" Eda begs him.

Nearly unconscious, Ed lies on the floor. Uncle Ted stops, looks at us with question, drops the broken chair leg, and leaves the room in fear and shame. Mom follows him, and I'm shocked to see the look on Mom's face. It's one of satisfaction.

Ed isn't moving. Eda rushes to him, sits down, and holds his head in her lap. She rubs his face with her hand, begging him, "Open your eyes. Please, open your eyes."

I am still frozen. This is too much for me to take in.

"Go get some water, Ariana. Hurry!"

I run to get it. From the balcony, I see Uncle Ted in the backyard smoking his cigarette and talking to Mom. I overhear him say,

"Woman, you crazy woman! You call me, drag me here at night, and lie to me that the boy talks back and destroys the house. I beat him up, and *then* I find out *he* didn't break the chair!"

"Well, he scratched the television set," Mom says nonchalantly.

"So what, you crazy woman! Maybe if you ever let him watch the damn TV, he wouldn't scratch it! That poor boy is going to hate me and I will never forgive myself! I almost killed him!" Uncle Ted whirls around and storms away from Mom and our house.

I rush to the kitchen, grab some water, and run back to Eda.

Ed is breathing heavily. He has scratches and bruises all over his face and body. He moves his head, but he can't talk.

As Mom walks in, I'm shocked to see that same look on her face.

"Go away!" she screams at Eda. "Don't worry, he won't die. Get up, boy! You were born only to kill me!"

She then orders us all to bed and to leave her alone. Eda gets up quickly, pulling Ed up with her, and asks me to help her make the beds. I'm happy to go to sleep, so I can pretend . . . pretend this day never existed.

Shooting Star

SEASONS CHANGE. Mom's tone of voice as she wakes us up in the morning is an indication of our day. Then again, that can change from good to bad in the blink of an eye. Once in a while, during summer or school holidays, Mom takes us to visit our relatives who live an hour away. Sometimes she takes us to the park on the outskirts of the mountain. She makes sandwiches and off we go.

On this hot summer day before the sun is out, Mom's bellowing jars us from our sleep. "Wake up and have your breakfast. I'm going grocery shopping."

We all get up except Josh. He sleeps much longer. We change and start putting away our bedding before we have our breakfast.

By the time Eda washes the dishes, Mom returns home. She sets the shopping bags on the balcony.

"Eda, take care of Josh while I make *ikra*," Mom says. "I want to finish grilling before the weather gets too hot."

"You're making *ikra*?" I cheer. "Can I help, Mom?"

"Yes, but keep quiet before I get mad."

I patiently wait and watch. Mom chops onion and garlic, which makes both of us cry. She puts them in a pan on top of a portable gas stove to sauté. Then she washes and pokes the eggplant, tomatoes, and green peppers, and lines them on the fiery hot grill. I keep close watch. Once cooked, they make a funny popping noise, and the steam comes out with a delicious smell.

"Mom, they're ready. Can I take them?"

"Keep your hands away. Do you want to burn yourself? Let me put them in water, then you can grab them by the stem to peel the skin off."

I do as Mom says. I separate the long stem from the eggplant and place it on my head. "Mom, look at my funny hat!"

"Okay. Enough. Put it down and don't be silly."

Soon, she mixes all the grilled vegetables with the sautéed onion and garlic, drenching them in olive oil. I can hardly wait!

Mom hands Ed some money and says, "Ed, go get some fresh bread. Hold it tightly in your hand so you don't lose it."

Ed runs to get the bread while I help Mom clean up. In the kitchen, she let the *ikra* cool off. The weather is hot now, so we stay inside. Ed comes back with bread, and for lunch, we have leftovers from the night before.

"After nap time, I will make *ikra* sandwiches and we'll go to the park."

"Really, Mom?" I ask.

"Yes. But if any of you makes me mad, not only will we not go, but I will punish all of you," she threatens.

We hold our breaths and get ready for a nap. We know Mom is serious. All three of us hope none of us will make a mistake. We don't worry about Josh though; Mom rarely gets mad at him, even if he doesn't sleep sometimes.

***

The sun is going down when Mom says, "Go get ready. Wear your old shoes, so you won't dirty your new ones."

We can't wait any longer and are ready in a flash!

Mom packs our sandwiches, and we walk a long way, which we don't mind it at all. We love to get out of our house.

The weather is cooling, and we are at the park where people stroll, children play, and vendors sell roasted corn on the cob, freshly salted walnuts, berries, and cotton candy. All of us run and roll in the grass; even Eda joins us.

"Watch out for Josh!" Mom says.

We chase each other and laugh so innocently, like there isn't a care in the world. We play, eat, and Mom even buys us cotton candy! She asks the man behind the machine to make one. He grabs a long wooden stick, and as he puts sugar in a large tray, he holds the stick close to it and twists. Soon a big, white ball of cotton candy is on the stick. He hands it to me, and we all share. Yum! Before I bite, it melts in my mouth. This is so funny to me. I love it.

***

We take the bus home. After several stops, we are at the end of our street. "Hurry up. Go wash your hands, change, and bring your bedding to the rooftop," Mom says as she takes Josh to her room to get him ready.

"We're sleeping on the roof?" Ed asks with excitement.

I smile. We enjoy sleeping there. It's so much fun!

The Knight of Nights has spread his cape of stars across the sky. Underneath is where we will sleep tonight. Mom keeps her water canteen and radio above her head, and Josh sleeps beside her. She listens to a story on the radio. I lie down between Ed and Eda, and all three of us, with our pointer fingers, trace the Warrior, the Big Bear, and the Milky Way. To make a wish, we look for a shooting star.

After a while, Ed elbows me. "Ariana, go get me some water."

Eda hears him and says, "Go get it yourself."

"Mom will get mad if I go," Ed whispers.

"Okay, I'll do it," I say. I tiptoe under the moonlight to where the canteen and water cup sit, above Mom's pillow.

"What the hell are you doing?" Mom asks firmly.

"Getting water for Ed," I answer, picking up the canteen and pouring water into the cup just a little too full. As I grab the cup, I spill a little on Mom's pillow. I bite my lip in fear and say, "I'm sorry, Mom. I'm sorry." Still holding the cup, I rush toward Ed and Eda. Ed grabs the water as Mom gets to me with her plastic slipper.

"I'm sorry, Mom," I beg.

"You rotten devil. You're good for nothing! You don't deserve to have a fun day," Mom barks and hits me with her slipper.

Eda grabs me in her arms, but she isn't safe from Mom's lashing either.

"Will you just shut up and let me rest?"

I lie on my bedding, weeping and holding tightly to Eda.

"Shut up, now! Enough!" Mom yells.

Eda holds her finger to her mouth to quiet me. Still sniffling with tears in my eyes, I look up to the sky, and I see a shooting star.

"Eda, I made a wish."

"What is it?"

"I wished for Papa to be our Mom, and for Mom to go away."

Eda cups my mouth.

***

Another endless summer is followed by an eventless fall, and a cold, boring winter. Christmas comes and goes without Papa or Santa. Just as Hamlet is the only one who has birthday parties, he is also the only one who Santa leaves presents for. Holding many wishes inside our hearts, we make it through.

1972–1975
A Bed Like Hamlet's

DURING THE SUMMER of my ninth birthday, we move to a new rental house in a three-story building. At first, I am happy. It is much bigger than our old one. Ed, Eda, and I share a bedroom, and since Mom bought us a bed set just like Hamlet's, I don't have to sleep on the floor anymore! Mom, Papa, and Josh share another one. We also have a big dining room and living room. The kitchen has a large window, from which I can look outside. We even have a bathroom shower and, best of all, we have an indoor toilet! Every room has new furniture, so Papa *must* be making more money.

Even with all the excitement and my cousins close by, in my heart, I miss Hamlet and our occasional play times.

Settling down in our new house takes several days of hard work for all of us, including Papa and my aunties. Once every room and closet is organized, Mom invites all my aunties and uncles over for a housewarming party. I get to play with my cousins: Nina, Rafael, Freddy, Irene, Anna, and Annie. I really like my new house!

After dinner, Papa asks Uncle Ted, "Is there a fitness club nearby?"

"Of course, the Armenian club, Ararat, is less than a thirty-minute walk. Why do you ask?"

"I want to sign Ariana up for gymnastics and Ed for judo or karate."

"That's a good idea!" Uncle Ted says.

With excitement, I run to Papa. "Is that where I'm going to practice gymnastics, Papa?"

"So, you just made this decision? And that's it?" Mom interrupts, frowning at Papa.

"Well, it is healthy, and it will keep them busy and fit."

"The decision is yours, Your Majesty," Mom replies as sarcastically as possible.

After everyone leaves, Papa calls Ed and me. As I jump in his lap, he says, "Ed, I will give you money and directions to the Ararat Club. Go there tomorrow and sign Ariana up for gymnastics and yourself for judo or karate."

I look at Papa in disbelief. "Papa, really? I'm going to get to be a gymnast?"

"Yes, *Shoonig*. I told you I'd do it as soon as I could."

I wrap my arms around Papa's neck. "Thank you, Papa."

***

Early the next morning, I shake Ed. "Are you awake, Ed?"

"Go away. Leave me alone, *esh*!"

I decide to let him be. I know if I call him one more time, he'll be all grumpy and mad. Instead, I go to the breakfast table.

"Is Ed awake?" Mom asks.

"Not yet, Mom," I reply.

"Go wake his lazy ass up!"

"Yes, Mom."

"Ed, get up. Mom is getting mad."

"Okay, already. I'll be there in a minute!"

I go back to the kitchen.

"Where's Eda?" Mom asks.

"She's in the bathroom."

"You lazy kids! It's seven o'clock in the morning! Five more minutes and there won't be any breakfast." She greets us every morning in the same way. Never nice.

"Mom, should I go wake Josh up?"

"No, let him sleep."

After breakfast, while Ed is getting ready to leave the house, I ask him, "Are you going to Ararat Club?"

"Yes, I'm going there, but I'm not going to sign you up."

"Why not, Ed?"

"Because I don't want to."

"But Papa told you to. Ed, please?"

He sniggers. "You whiny baby. Wa, wa, wa!"

"Will you sign me up?"

"Yes, *esh*."

Not even Mom can spoil my excitement. I'm so happy I can't control myself. I go out to our backyard. To celebrate, I jump rope and cheer. I already feel like a gymnast!

On My Team

ED AND I WALK TOWARD the fitness club. Sporadically, we talk, but mostly I just take in my surroundings.

"There it is, you see?" Ed says. "Look, there is the sign that says Ararat."

"Oh, yes! Now I see it!"

We walk through an old gray wooden door and head down two steps into a big courtyard. Several brick buildings surround us. One is a small deli and the others house indoor activity centers and offices.

Ed directs me to the building where I will meet with my coach. As soon as we find him, Ed leaves. "I'll be back to get you. Just stay here," Ed says as he walks away.

"Hello," a young man says to me. "My name is Tadeous, but you can call me Tatool. I am the gymnastics coach. What is your name and how old are you?"

"Um, I am Ariana, and I am nine years old."

"Have you ever been on a team or played any sports at all?" Tatool asks.

"No, sir, not ever. This is my first time."

"Well then, let's try some moves and see what you've got."

He leads me to an area where the blue mats are laid on the floor. Some are old and ripped, and some are new.

"Okay, now show me if you can touch the floor with your fingertips without bending your knees."

I do exactly as he commands.

Nodding, he asks, "Can you touch your chin to your knees?"

I do that, too.

With raised eyebrows, Tatool asks me, "Can you lie down and pose a bridge for me?"

I do that, too.

"Very impressive! Now I need you to run around this room and I will time you. Are you ready?"

I nod.

"Get ready, set, go!"

I run as fast as I've ever run before. I stop only when my coach tells me to. I am breathless and eager for what he'll say next. He looks at me, taps my shoulder, and says, "Very good! I think you have what it takes. I'd love to have you on my team."

"Oh, thank you, sir!" I cheerfully reply. I can't wait to give this news to Papa! "When can I start?"

"You can stay and practice today if you want. I have extra gymnastics shoes for you to borrow, but you'll still need to go and buy your own."

"Yes, sir. Thank you. I would like that."

Tatool introduces me to all the other girls. Most of them are much older and have been on the team for many years. I'm the youngest and the newest. My excitement is hard to contain. I begin to practice!

Time flies by. It's dark outside and everyone is ready to leave. Ed arrives and Tatool tells him, "Bring her three times a week at six o'clock sharp. Practice ends at nine. She needs gymnastics shoes and a black leotard. I'll give you the address and name of the store where you can find them. And by the way, I must tell you, your sister is very talented."

"Thank you, sir. I will bring her with me since I myself am in karate." Ed thanks Tatool and we leave together.

As we walk home, my entire body is jittery, but I am so excited!

When we arrive, Papa and Eda are watching the news. I turn to Papa and with a huge grin on my face, I say, "I made the team!"

Papa praises me. "Good job, my daughter! I knew you could do it!"

"Yes, Papa, the coach says she is very talented, and she needs to have her own leotard and gymnastics shoes," says Ed.

"Okay, your mom will buy them for you," Papa says and turns to Mom. "Liz, buy her the stuff she needs."

Mom carelessly shakes her head and states, "If I have time."

I get the feeling that she won't.

Papa looks to Ed. "Son, you have more time. You can take your sister and get her what she needs."

"Yes, Papa. I will," he replies.

The next day, Ed and I go shopping. I can't believe I'm going to be a gymnast!

***

Days, weeks, and month pass. I work hard three times a week, three intense hours every time. A typical practice routine includes running laps around the gym, push-ups, sit-ups, "wheelbarrow" walking, and working on our splits. But the most difficult of all is hanging from a pull-up bar and bringing my legs to a ninety-degree angle. Sometimes my body hurts so much I can't even sleep. As if my soreness isn't enough, I also have to wash my leotard each night after practice. Mom refuses to touch my workout clothes. She once told me, "If you want to be a gymnast, you'll have to wash your own stinky clothes."

But nothing can keep me from loving gymnastics. I don't care how hard it is.

After a year, Tatool announces, "In the next few months, some of you will enter the city championship. I will announce your names. If you hear yours, you've been chosen for the competition."

He proceeds to read his list. When I hear "Ariana," I look at Tatool and my teammates, who all cheer wildly for me.

"Me?" I ask, pointing to myself.

"Yes, you!" Tatool says.

I can't believe it! My dream has come true.

***

For the next six months, the practice is extremely difficult. Tatool has even added an extra day's practice.

"You all have to work much harder. You ladies will represent your city, yourself, and me. I will give you your individual programs based on your abilities. You must memorize the moves and master them."

I can hardly wait for my program! Ever since I told Mom I'd be competing, she has not said a single word. But she can't quell my excitement!

Tatool gives me my program.

Oh boy! But as I review it, I see it looks difficult.

Tatool asks me, "Are you nervous, Ariana?"

"Yes, I am. It looks pretty hard."

"Don't worry. You have plenty of time to practice. And with your talent, I'm certain you can do this."

Tatool helps me learn and improve. Sometimes he raises his voice at me, but on the other hand, he also tells me I do a great job. Many times I tumble or fall, but every day, I get better. I have floor, beam, and vault programs. The floor routine is the easiest. I get to do all my jumps, cartwheels, and splits on the mat.

The beam routine is a different story. At the beginning, it is only a few inches above the ground. I walk on it, turn around, do the splits, jump, and roll. Tatool has designated Maria, one of the oldest teammates, to help me. It wasn't long before I graduated to the tall beam, since poor Maria injured her foot and can't compete. At first, it looks intimidating, but she helps me mount it with a jump and both my feet together. I jump and set my knees on the beam, twist my legs open sideways, then straight, and hold my balance upon my hands perfectly still, then roll and stand up. I must have fallen a hundred times trying to master this move. Bruised or hurt, I always get up and continue day after day.

Sometimes, after practice, despite being tired, I wait a long time for Ed to pick me up. Usually, it's dark and late at night. Ed likes to hang out with his friends after his karate practice, so he often loses track of time.

When we get home after a long walk, I'm sore and nauseous, and, of course, I still have to wash my leotard. After most practices, I have to deal with Mom's madness and bitter comments.

Tonight, she yells at me threateningly, "It's the last time you'll go to practice. You think you'll be a gymnast? You are nothing but a loser. You'll never amount to anything."

Mom's words break my heart. I cry myself to sleep, but something inside keeps me going.

In the Stands

ON THE BUS RIDE to the opening ceremony, we check each other's braided hair to make sure it looks good. Some of the older teammates brought eye shadow and lipstick along.

Maria, who will still walk with us today, says to me, "You should put some lipstick on, Ariana."

I giggle and bashfully say, "I don't have any. And if my mom finds out, she'll get really mad."

"Oh, come on. She won't notice your lipstick from a distance."

"Well, my mom won't be there to watch me anyway."

"What? Are you sure? Everyone's families will be there to cheer for all of us."

As soon as she finishes her sentence, Tatool announces, "We're here!" Popping up from our seats, we just about jump out of our skin. "Showtime, ladies!" All smiles as we get off the bus, Tatool hands us our name tags, then we get in a straight line and follow him to a field in an enormous brand-new stadium.

In a straight line, we follow him to a field in an enormous brand-new stadium. I've never been in a stadium before! As I scan the rows and rows filled with thousands of people, I realize I'm trembling.

My teammates try hard to find their families in the stands. Well, I don't have that problem; no one is here for me.

The national anthem begins to play as we stand up tall. My heart pounds as we march. Shockeh and Maggie, two of my teammates, lead us to the front row of our lineup carrying a big banner with "Ararat" proudly written on it. With our braided hair, blue leotards, and white gymnastics shoes, each of us carries a small flag representing our team. The audience cheers, applauds, and whistles.

After the marching, a big festival takes place with games, good food, and my favorite: roasted corn! My teammates find their families, as I stand alone, feeling like an orphan. I do have some money Papa gave me hidden inside my white sock. Part of me wants to go and buy some roasted corn, but I'm too shy. Someone taps on my shoulder from behind and I spin around. "Oh, Maria. It's you!"

"I want to introduce you to my parents, Ariana. I've told them all about you," she insists.

"Okay, let's go!"

"There they are!" Maria points, grabbing my hand, and hurries me over to them. "Mom, Dad, this is my friend Ariana."

"Well, hello, Ariana. How are you? We've heard you'll be performing tomorrow," her mother kindly says to me.

Bashfully, I say, "Hello, fine, and yes."

Afterward, I hang out with Maria and her family until it's time to head back to the bus and our neighborhood gymnasium to be picked up by our families.

Tatool says, "You ladies did great! You were very organized and neat. After you get home, make sure to rest and do a lot of stretching. Tomorrow is our big day! Be on time. Arrive three hours before your competition."

I listen and carefully plan it all out in my head.

As we get back to the gym, everyone leaves except for me. I'm the last one, alone in the dark, and it's well past ten.

"Who's supposed to pick you up?" Tatool asks, very concerned.

"My brother, Ed," I reply with worry.

"All right, I'll stay here with you until he comes."

"Thank you, Tatool." I am trying my best not to cry.

"So tell me, how many siblings do you have?"

"I have two brothers and one sister."

We continue to talk about my family, but I think Tatool is tired and worried for me. He's probably just trying to keep my mind busy.

"Did all of your family come today to watch the opening ceremony?" Tatool peers into my eyes, searching for the truth.

I put my head down, still in my leotard and gymnastics shoes, and drag my toes on the cement. Hesitantly, I reply, "No, sir, they didn't come."

"Don't drag your foot on the cement, Ariana. You'll scrape your shoes," he admonishes, gently tapping my shoulder. "Where are your extra shoes? You can't walk on these shoes to get home."

"Ed has my bag."

Tatool looks at his watch. One hour has already passed. "I think I should take you home. It's too late. Are you sure he's going to pick you up?"

I look at Tatool pleadingly with no answer.

"Well, let me take you home. I have my car parked here."

"But my mom gets mad."

"It's better than staying here on the street. I hope your brother isn't lost," he says.

The entire drive home I am worried and scared. *What will happen when I get home? Will Mom be mad? Will she hit me? And where is Ed?*

We reach my neighborhood, which is very close to Tatool's house. We just figured this out earlier.

At my house, Tatool rings the bell. Mom swings the door open angrily. "Where have you been?!" she screams in my face.

Tatool steps forward. "Hello, ma'am."

"Oh, I'm sorry. I didn't realize you were here. I was worried sick for her," she says, pointing at me. "Where's Ed?"

Before I can reply, Tatool answers, "Well, ma'am, I don't know. That's why I brought her home. It's late."

"Thank you, sir."

"No problem, ma'am. Good night, Ariana. See you tomorrow at the competition. Don't be late. Your program is at six."

I wave at him, then walk into the house. Before I can close the door, Mom slaps me across the face. "Where the hell have you been?! Where is Ed?"

"I don't know, Mom."

I put my hand on my cheek as tears roll down my face. Mom keeps yelling.

Eda wakes up and says, "What is it, Mom? What's going on?"

"Where the hell is your damn brother?"

As if on cue, Ed walks in with a fearful look in his eyes.

"Where the hell have you been, you jerk?" She throws her slipper at him.

I cringe against the wall, crying, as Eda tries to calm Mom down.

"I'm sorry, Mom. I was with my friends and I lost track of time."

"You have nothing better to do than hang out with your faggot friends!"

"Here we go again. Mom, don't call me names!" Ed counters, standing his ground.

Mom is mad, but she also has that look on her face. The same look she gives when we are hurt.

Ed storms off to the bedroom and I follow.

No one says a word as we drift off to sleep.

The Big Day

DESPITE THE BITTER MEMORY of last night, I wake up and begin stretching and practicing my routine. I organize my gym bag at least a hundred times during the day. Every once in a while, I ask Eda to watch me do the splits or even a cartwheel.

"You look great with every move you make. I think you'll have a fantastic performance."

Eda's encouraging words give me hope and strength. I can hardly keep my excitement contained!

Competition day is finally here! I take my shower, brush and braid my hair, and check my gym bag, again. I walk through and repeat my moves over and over in my head, practicing on our rug, counting my steps, turning, even pretending to jump.

Mom ignores me completely as Eda helps her get dessert ready for afternoon coffee with my aunts. I check the clock on the wall—two o'clock. Almost time!

Running to the kitchen, I announce, "I'm ready, Mom! It's time to go!"

Mom looks at me. "Where?"

"Mom, it's my competition day, remember? I don't want to be late."

"What the hell are you talking about? You aren't going anywhere!"

"But, but, it's my competition day, Mom?" I simply cannot bear it if she doesn't let me go. "Mom, please? My program is at six. Tatool is waiting for me," I plead, my heart shattering with realization.

"Get lost, you little brat! And shut up!" Mom yells, her eyes dark voids of hate.

I go to my bedroom, where I kneel near my bed and hide my face in my palms. I don't know how long I cry before I get up the courage to go to Mom once again.

Clearly afraid, tears in my eyes, I ask, "Why can't I go? I am begging, Mom."

She turns around and says, "Because I said so. You are not allowed to go. End of story."

Once more, I see that look on her face. I look to Eda, whose eyes say, "I'm so sorry."

Retreating to my bedroom, I take out my gymnastics shoes and hold them tightly to my chest. Sobbing, I sit on my bedroom floor, wrapped in a blanket of sorrow. I am crushed.

Mom's bitter words replay in my mind. "You are nothing but a loser. You are nobody." She carved her words into my soul today.

When I can't cry anymore, I dab my eyes and place the hurt in my box of memories.

And the music plays in my head.

And I perform my program perfectly.

Ice Cream

ALL SUMMER AND FALL, I try to accept the bitter truth that I will never be a gymnast. Now, it's winter. After I've been sick one too many times, Mom takes me to an ear, nose, and throat specialist.

"Ariana, go get ready. I'm taking you to a new doctor."

"But my throat only hurts a little bit."

"That's why we are going, so it won't get worse."

I put on my orange dress and leggings, brush my hair, and put it in a half ponytail. Once I pile on my boots and coat, I'm ready to go.

After a fifteen-minute walk, we get to the doctor's office. Sitting in the waiting room makes me nervous. Mom gives my name and some money to a lady behind a desk.

Soon, a nurse comes with her long, white coat and calls, "Ariana Mikaelian."

Mom gets up, pulling my hand. "Yes, that's my daughter."

The nurse says, "Follow me this way."

We do.

"You sit here on the table," she says, pointing. Then she puts the thermometer under my tongue. I hate it! She says, "It looks like you have a low-grade fever."

"Here we go again," Mom murmurs. "She is always sick. I have no life, miss." Mom complains until there is a knock on the door. A big man, also wearing a long white coat and a stethoscope around his neck, walks in.

"Hello, Doctor," Mom greets, and I do the same.

"Hello," he says in a dry, abrupt tone. "So, what is the problem?"

First the nurse shows him the chart and says, "She has a low-grade fever."

The doctor comes close to me, checks my lungs and heart, and says, "Open your mouth." As I do, he puts a metal stick on my tongue, and with the other hand, holds a small flashlight inside my mouth, until I start gagging and coughing. In a harsh tone, he says, "What's wrong with you?"

A few teardrops roll down my face, but I keep quiet.

The doctor turns to Mom and says, "She has tonsillitis, and if this is occurring often, we need to remove her tonsils."

Panicking, I ask, "Is that going to hurt?"

The nurse, who has been quiet until now, says, "You won't feel anything. And after surgery, you can have ice cream." Her answer was good but not convincing.

Mom looks at the doctor and says, "Sir, she gets sick at least twice a month. I am all alone with three other children at home. It is impossible for me to take care of them when she is constantly sick."

The look on the doctor's face shows indifference.

"Nurse, take this girl to the lab and run some blood work," he orders.

Mom asks, "What is going to happen? When will you do this surgery?"

"As soon as I see the lab results. Bring her back next week. Meanwhile, get this prescription filled and start her on this antibiotic to clear the infection."

I wait for somebody to tell me what's going on, but that doesn't happen.

At the follow-up appointment with the doctor, he checks my test results, and I am scheduled for surgery.

"Since the hospital is too far, and your father is not home, as usual, I will ask Uncle Eddie to take us for your surgery," Mom says.

"Yay!" I reply, knowing I will see my Uncle Eddie, Mom's youngest brother, who is small-framed, kind, funny, and makes me happy. For a moment, I forget about the surgery.

"When will Uncle Eddie come?"

"Tomorrow, by five in the morning."

Ed is watching a science program on TV, Josh quietly paints in his coloring book, and Eda dutifully sets the dinner table.

"That's early," Ed says. "Is Uncle Eddie going to stay here awhile?"

"No. He is just picking us up," Mom answers.

Disappointed, Ed returns to the TV.

***

"Wake up, Ariana."

I open my eyes, looking out the window between the gap of the curtains. It's still dark. I climb down off my bed and get ready. My stomach growls since I wasn't allowed to have dinner last night or breakfast today, but I am excited to see my Uncle Eddie. From the kitchen window, I notice the snow.

"Are you ready, Ariana?"

"Mom, look! It's snowing!"

"I know. I asked you if you're ready."

"Yes, I am."

"Put your hat and coat on. It's very cold outside."

As I put them on, I hear a honking. "Mom, is it him? Is Uncle Eddie here?"

"Yes. Hurry up. Let's go."

It's windy, and snow is coming down hard. As we get in the car, Uncle Eddie starts cracking jokes, even about the weather. He makes me laugh, and I forget about where we are going.

It takes a while for us to get to the hospital. Once we arrive, I get checked in and a nurse takes me to a room, changes my clothes into a hospital gown, and says, "Lay down here and watch TV until the doctor arrives."

"Mom, I'm hungry," I say.

"I know. After the surgery, you will have ice cream. Now close your eyes and sleep a little."

I stare out the window, then back to the TV screen. I fall asleep thinking about ice cream.

A nurse wakes me up. "It's time. The doctor is here. Get up and follow me."

I climb off the bed, wearing a hospital gown way too big for me. I look at Mom and ask, "Aren't you coming?"

The nurse answers, "No, she will wait here for you."

Confused and scared, I follow the nurse to a big, cold room. I feel lonely, and want desperately to leave and run home. I don't like it here.

"Sit there," the nurse orders as she points to a chair at the end of the room. Afraid and shivering, I follow her orders and sit on a cold, metal chair.

The doctor comes in wearing surgical gloves and the nurse follows behind him with a rolling tray full of scary-looking instruments and a big syringe with a long needle.

"Open your mouth big and wide," the doctor says to me. "Hold her hands and her head, so she can't move," he tells the nurse.

She follows his orders, and I feel like I'm about to pass out. Tears roll down my cheeks as he sticks the big syringe in my throat. The excruciating pain makes me move.

"Be still!" he yells.

All I can think about is how much I want to get out of here.

The doctor carries on a conversation with the nurse. "The traffic is so bad today with this snow. That's why I arrived late. I have to rush to catch up with my schedule." As he is talking, he grabs a scissor-like instrument, puts it to my throat, and cuts. I scream, feeling nauseous.

"Shut up!" he yells, and he hits me in my chest, pushing me back to the chair. Tears fall freely as I gag. He then goes in for the next cut. I don't feel this one, but I can hear the sound of it. Next, he sticks a curved needle with a long, black thread in my mouth and shoves it into my throat.

With the help of the nurse, I walk to my hospital room, weak and tired, and fall asleep.

Mom's voice wakes me up, and I see the angry doctor's face talking to Mom. "The surgery went well. If she doesn't have bleeding, you can take her home in a few hours. Make her soup or mashed potatoes."

"No ice cream?" Mom asks.

"No," he replies. "That's not in my orders." Then he grabs a piece of gauze and holds it in front of my mouth. "Spit in this," he orders. It hurts my throat so bad I can hardly spit, but there is no blood. "Good. I will sign the release form, and you can leave."

***

We arrive home by taxi. Tired and hungry, I change into my pajamas. Worn out and in lots of pain, I sleep for a while.

When I wake up, Mom says, "I made you some chicken soup. Have some."

It smells so good, but it hurts to swallow, so I stop eating. My aunties arrive to visit me, and Mom begins *her* story. "It was so hard for me to sit in the waiting room. I kept praying and crying. All the nurses tried to comfort me, but I just couldn't relax. There is always something to worry me. I guess I'm just an unlucky woman."

"You are not unlucky. This happens all the time," Auntie Emma says.

"No. It happens to me more than anyone," Mom replies with assertion. Listening to Mom and my aunties' conversation, I have to wonder which one of us had the horrifying experience.

Not Too Far

EDA LOOKS THROUGH the newspaper, running her finger over the pages as if she's searching for something. I sit next to her at the table, bent over on my elbows with hands under my chin, staring at her. I've always admired her beauty—long, shiny hair, beautifully shaped nose, and slim, perfect figure—and want to be just like her when I'm older.

"What are you looking for, Eda?"

"I'm trying to find a place where I can go to learn English. I need something to do. I feel like I'm rotting at home." Eda points. "Here it is: English Speaking and Grammar School."

"Where, Eda?"

"Look here." Eda indicates the ad.

With curiosity, I read it.

"When Papa comes home, I'll ask him. I'm sure he'll agree to it!" Eda says.

At first, I thought Eda was talking to me, but now I see she's really talking to herself.

"Eda, you look silly!"

"Why, Ariana?"

"Well, you sound like you're talking to yourself. Blah, blah, blah."

We giggle together.

Mom comes home with groceries and Josh runs to her with his toy car in hand. "What are you two doing? Come and help me," Mom orders.

Eda and I rush over to her. As we help, Eda braces herself and asks, "Mom, may I go to this English summer school?" Then quickly adds, "It's during the evenings and not too expensive."

"Why in the world would you want English lessons?"

Eda softly replies, "I think it will give me something to do."

"You'll have to ask your father," Mom says emotionlessly.

Eda and I look at each other. Here we go, again. Ed, Eda, and I are all too familiar with this kind of answer. Usually when Mom answers like that, she wants to end the conversation. Even if Papa agrees, somehow, she will get her way.

*****

Papa comes home a few days later.

Eda is determined to go to English summer school and asks him, "Papa, I found this school program. It's in the evenings and the place isn't too far. I can walk there."

"Slow down, my daughter," Papa says. "What school are you talking about?"

"Oh, sorry, Papa. It's a school with English classes," she explains.

"Well, how much does it cost?"

"I know it's not expensive, Papa."

"Then you may go."

"Thank you, Papa!" Eda's face is all bright and happy.

Mom is a quiet storm brewing.

Papa asks her, "Don't you think it's a good idea, Liz?"

"Who cares about my opinion? You make the decision. Why even bother to ask me?"

"It's good to have an education," Papa replies. "Here, Eda. Take this and go sign up." And he hands her some money.

Mom is *not* happy.

***

The next morning, I ask Eda, "Can I go with you?"

"Yes," she answers.

"Are we going now?"

"No, not now. We'll go this afternoon. Help me clean the house and do our chores so Mom won't get upset."

I do, and then play some with Josh. He's my playmate when Eda isn't around or she's helping Mom. We play "house," as I wait for afternoon.

Finally, Eda comes to me. "Come, let's fix your hair."

"Is it time to go?" I ask, sitting in the kitchen chair.

"Yes."

She puts my hair in a high ponytail, ties it with a white ribbon, and off we go.

As soon as we leave the house, I say, "Eda, I think Mom really doesn't want you to go."

"I don't care," she says.

We've been walking for a while, and the neighborhood looks unfamiliar to me. I spot a big building with a huge picture above it, showing a man sitting on a horse and holding a lasso, with cows all around him.

"Look, Eda! There's a cinema! Can we go there?"

"No. But someday, I will take you."

"Eda, why doesn't Mom take us to see a movie?"

"Because she doesn't like it."

"The only time I've seen a movie was when Papa took us."

"You remember that? You were so little, Ariana."

With a smile, I say, "I even remember the name of the movie. It was *Little Rita*, and it was an American movie. The girl in it could shoot just about any target."

"Whoa, Ariana! You really surprise me!"

Once we pass the theater, Eda says, "Look, Ariana. We're almost there. Look!" she says, pointing at a big black and yellow neon sign.

"Yes, I see it!" We arrive at the building and walk inside. Eda leads me upstairs to the office, where she begins talking to the person who I think must be in charge.

I wait patiently for some time. Then, when I least expect it, I hear my name. "Ariana, let's go."

Reaching for Eda's hand, I ask, "Are you already done?"

"Yes, of course. Let's go now," she says.

"My legs are so tired, Eda. You told Mom and Papa it wasn't really far."

"Never mind what I said. If I said it was far, Papa wouldn't let me go."

"You're right."

"Don't you say anything."

"Of course not, Eda." I never tell on Ed or Eda, even when Mom interrogates me.

***

After the long hike, we arrive home. Papa is chit-chatting with Ed and teaching Josh how to play chess.

"Hello, Papa," Eda and I chime.

Eda announces, "Papa, I signed up for the classes and I'll start next week!"

"Well, that's great!" Papa says supportively.

I think I'm more anxious than Eda for her classes to start.

Mom says not a word, her eyes cutting daggers.

Same Path

LOOKING BEAUTIFUL IN HER denim skirt and pale pink shirt, Eda puts on a little mascara and lipstick, which she keeps hidden in her bag. It's been two weeks since she began her English summer school classes, and she is glowing.

"Oh, Ariana, you have to go to these classes when you're older! You learn so much. Plus, all the students are smart and eager to learn. It isn't boring at all!" She is so enthusiastic. "There's this boy and I know he likes me."

I giggle with my eyes wide open. "Oh, my gosh, Eda! If Mom finds out, she'll kill you!"

"How is she going to find out? Anyway, I'm not doing anything bad. Poor guy keeps asking me if I'll go for coffee or ice cream, and I keep saying no. I just tell him he can walk with me to the edge of our neighborhood, and that's all."

"That's nice, Eda, but I still worry for you. I know Mom doesn't want us to talk to boys. But you're right. How would she find out?"

***

A few days later, out of the blue, before it's time for Eda to get home, Mom decides to take Josh and me for a stroll.

"Mom, where are we going? Is it far?"

"Maybe. I'm not sure," she answers.

The path we take seems familiar.

"Mom, I think this is how Eda goes to school. Am I right?"

With an evil look, she answers, "Yes, it is, you little bitch. You keep secrets from me. I will kill the both of you!" Mom threatens furiously.

Little did I know she had heard Eda telling me about her boyfriend.

As we get closer to Eda's school, I am dying inside. I attempt to distance myself from Mom, but all I can picture is Eda's face.

Then there she is, walking toward us with a boy classmate, but she hasn't seen Mom or me yet. I want to run to her and save her. I want to separate her from him.

Mom grabs my hand and squeezes my wrist, pulling me closer to her. I gasp.

That's when Eda glances up and sees us. Her books clutched to her chest, she stops and tells the boy, "Go!" as she distances herself from him.

With a puzzled look on his face, he turns and walks away.

Mom reaches Eda and slaps her right there in the street! Humiliated, Eda puts her head down, as people passing by stare and walk away.

As we hurriedly walk home, with Eda ahead of us, Mom keeps me back, grabbing my arm with a vise-like grip, and hisses, "If you take one step closer to her, I'm gonna break your arm and hurt you so bad you'll never forget!"

I know Eda is crying. I want to get close to her, hold her hand, and comfort her like she always does for me.

Reaching our home, I know something bad is about to happen. Eda heads to the bedroom, with Mom yelling at her, "You bitch! You whore!"

I forget about Josh and run after Eda to the bedroom, but Mom pushes me away.

"What, you little whore? Is your sister teaching you all these things?" Mom spits at me, then turns her rage on Eda.

"Mom, I swear I haven't done anything," Eda cries. "That boy is my classmate. We were just walking home."

As she screams horrid vulgarity at my sweet sister, Mom takes Eda's books, one at a time, and begins ripping them apart. All I can do is cry.

"Mom, please don't," Eda sobs, standing near the wall.

With wild-eyes, Mom lunges at Eda, grabs the hair on each side of her head, and bashes it into the brick wall. The hair-raising sound of her head pounding against the wall echoes in my ears.

My eyes stop tearing, my heart stops beating. I am terrorized to see the color drain from my sister's face, her eyes roll back, and body go limp as she slides down to the floor.

"Mom! She's dead!" I scream and fall to my knees. "Eda, Eda, wake up!" I scream, rushing to Eda's side, and reach for her foot, desperately trying to shake her awake. She doesn't respond.

"Get away! Get away!" Mom screams at me. Running to the backyard, she returns with the water hose, dragging it into the room, and drenches Eda with it. Abruptly, she drops it, wild-eyed. Water is everywhere. She grabs ahold of Eda's shoulders, shaking her unmercifully. Eda is unresponsive, limp as a rag doll.

"Wake up, Eda! Please!" I beg.

That's when Mom begins slapping her. Eda barely opens her eyes and gasps for air. *Thank God!*

Mom snaps, realizing the rug is soaking wet, and roars at me, "Hurry up! Get the hose out of here!"

I haul the hose to the backyard and rush back inside to check on Eda. Mom tries to dry Eda's body and hair, and begins changing her wet clothes.

I hear Josh crying in the other room, so I run and take him to Mom's bedroom. I pat and comfort him until he falls asleep.

I am in shock. I cannot understand what just happened to my sister.

After I hear Mom leave her room, I tip-toe over and lie down with Eda. Weeping quietly, I hold her and pray, "My dear Jesus, please help Eda. Help her to get well." Caressing my sister's hand, I fall asleep.

***

Mom's commanding voice wakes me the next morning. "Get up!" she orders angrily, approaching Eda's bed. I'm afraid she'll hit her again, but she only rolls Eda over, who only makes a weak noise. I don't know where she's hurt.

Eda doesn't get up all day, not even to eat. A couple of times, in a weak voice, she whispers, "My head hurts," and Mom gives her an aspirin.

I wish I could make her feel better. I want to tell her I didn't tell Mom about her classmate; that I didn't know Mom was coming to her English school; that I'm sorry I wasn't able to stop Mom from hurting her.

Waiting Is the Hardest Part

I WAS BORN DURING the last month of winter, and today, after so many years, Mom tells me I can have a birthday party! I can't believe what I'm hearing.

"Why are you staring at me, Ariana? What's wrong with you?"

"Nothing, Mom. I can't believe—You mean I can have a birthday party? I can have my classmates over to our house?"

"Yes, you can, but only a few. And I will invite all of your cousins and aunts."

"Thank you so much, Mom!"

I keep thinking what my party will be like since I've never had one before. I'm going to be thirteen years old and have my very first birthday party!

Eda comes home from grocery shopping for Mom. I run to her. "Eda, Eda, Mom just told me I'm going to have a birthday party!"

"Really? How'd that happen?" She is stunned.

"I don't care, Eda. All I do care about is that I can have my friends and cousins over." I am beside myself. "Eda, will you help me? I don't know what to do."

"Well, you need to invite your friends. I think Mom will invite our cousins and aunts. And also, you need some kind of board game, a birthday cake, fruit, tea, and coffee," she explains.

"Oh, Eda, I can't wait! I'm so excited!"

"I know! I'm excited for you. You have a few days. Remember when you go to school tomorrow, invite your friends and write down our home address for them."

"I will!" The faces of my friends flash before my eyes. *Who shall I invite??*

I go to bed with so many thoughts in my head. I fall asleep dreaming of a happy, beautiful birthday party with all my friends from school and my cousins. We play a board game and then my best friend, Shady, suggests we play Musical Chairs. We dance and, at last, Mom brings me this big birthday cake with colorful candles. I blow them all out with just one blow! And the best part? I have so many presents to open!

***

It seems I had just closed my eyes when I hear Mom's voice in my ear. "Wake up! Wake up! You'll be late for school!"

I jump up and realize it was only a dream.

After a quick breakfast, I ask Mom, "Will you invite my cousins?"

"Yes, today," she answers curtly.

Beaming, I walk to school. Midway, I meet Irene, Anna, and Nina. I tell them about my birthday party on Saturday. When I get to school, I invite my friends, including my good friend Shady, who is Persian. Waiting is the hardest part!

***

At last, it's Saturday. Mom bakes a cake for me and decorates it with powdered sugar. Eda and I clean the house, then I get ready.

I brush my hair, put on my navy-and-red pleated skirt and red woven sweater, and wait for everyone to arrive at four. Time passes s-l-o-w-l-y. I keep checking my hair and clothes. I constantly go to the kitchen and hop up on the chair to look out the window to the street. No one is there. I decide to go check on my board game to make sure it's in a good place and that Josh hasn't touched it. I check the window once more.

It's five o'clock.

"Eda, don't you think the guests should be here by now?"

"Maybe they're running late," Eda comforts. "Did you give our address to your friends?"

"Yes, but I don't know why no one is here." As I finish my sentence, the doorbell rings. I run to the door.

"Oh, hi, Shady. Come on in!" She enters and hands me a small box wrapped in colorful wrapping paper. I hurry and rip the wrapping paper open. My goodness, it's a fancy purple pencil box! Inside are a few pencils and a pink eraser that smells so good! I take the eraser and hold it under my nose, inhaling with my eyes closed. "Oh, it smells like strawberries!" I do this a few more times before I put it back in the box. *And my new fancy pencil box has a built-in sharpener!* I take it to Mom and Eda so excited!

Again, I notice none of my cousins are here. Turning around, I go back to Shady. "Thank you for my wonderful present."

We start to play and snack on some fruit. The worry is eating at my soul.

With a blank expression on her face, Mom silently hands Shady and me a piece of cake.

Shady says, "Don't you blow out candles on your birthday?"

"I don't know. I think my mom forgot about it."

When Shady and I finish eating our cake, she sets her plate down and politely says, "It's getting late. I must be getting home." She doesn't know what else to do and leaves.

It's past seven. My birthday party ends with none of my cousins showing up. And even though I was expecting fifteen guests in all, only one came.

Once more, I go to the kitchen, stand on the chair near the window, crack it open, and look outside to see snow falling. I look to the street. No one is there. Disappointed and confused, I climb down. "Mom, how come nobody came to my birthday party?" Not expecting an answer, I turn and shuffle to my bedroom. *Why didn't my cousins show up? Did Mom even invite them at all?*

I grab my new pencil box, take out the strawberry-smelling eraser, stick it to my nose, and give thanks.

I Think I Can!

THE SHAH'S NEW RULE encourages women to join the military. Eda finds this out through the afternoon newspaper.

"Look at this," Eda says, pointing at an article.

"What is it, Eda?"

"Here it says all women aged eighteen to thirty-five must sign up for military service."

"Really, Eda? You get to be a soldier?"

"Yes, Ariana! Can you believe it?" As I stare at my sister, her eyes light up.

"Do you think Papa will let you join the army?"

"Well, here it says if I don't sign up, there will be mandatory drafting."

As Eda and I read the newspaper, Papa comes home.

"Hi, Papa!" we both say. I run to shake hands with him.

"Hello, *Baless*." He returns my handshake and caresses Eda's long silky hair. "What are you two girls doing?"

"Papa, have you heard the Shah's new rule?" Eda asks.

"What rule? Now he comes up with new rules? What good has he done with his old ones that he now has new ones?" Papa murmurs.

"Papa, this is for real. There is a call to duty for women, and signing is mandatory."

"Ha, there is no such thing! Wishful thinking. Iran is not ready for it."

"But Papa, listen. All women aged eighteen to thirty-five have to sign up within two months. If not, their signing will be mandatory," Eda says seriously. "This is not a joke."

As Eda finishes her sentence, I carry on, "Papa, won't it be interesting to see Eda in a uniform?"

"No. Eda isn't going anywhere."

"Papa, I have to sign up," Eda insists.

"No, you don't."

"But if I don't, I'll get in trouble!"

"*Baless*, this is not going to take place. And don't worry, in a week or two, they will come up with some kind of excuse and dismiss the rule."

"You think so, Papa?" I ask.

"Of course, *Baless*. Now let's eat something. I'm starving. By the way, where is your mother?"

"She'll be home soon. She went to visit Auntie Emma," Eda replies.

Several weeks pass and the news gets even more serious. Eda keeps updated by reading the newspaper every day. Even I am curious to see what will happen.

Soon, an announcement is made that those who haven't signed up by the end of the month will be prosecuted.

"Mom, I must sign up. I don't want to get in trouble. Papa keeps saying they will dismiss the rule, but obviously, it isn't going to happen."

"Okay then, go and take care of it."

Eda quickly grabs her documents, along with the address for the military office, and heads out the door.

***

Eda is gone for almost the entire afternoon. When she gets home, I'm working on my latest crossword puzzle.

"Hi," Eda says, dragging her feet.

"Hi, Eda. You look tired."

"I'm exhausted. I stood in line for hours."

Mom walks in from her bedroom. "So, what happened?" she demands.

"Well, since I was late for signing, I have to join the military. For me, it's mandatory. I must go," Eda answers.

"Yay, Eda! You'll get to wear a soldier's uniform." Not knowing the details of what's in store for Eda, I'm happy for her. I know she really wants to join; not because she cares about being in the military, but because she'll be getting away from Mom.

"Just what exactly will you be doing?" Mom asks angrily.

"I don't know the details, Mom. All I do know is I have to be at the military base here in town at the end of the month along with some of my personal items. They gave me a list."

"I guess that means you won't be coming home?" Mom huffs.

"No," Eda says. "For the first six months, I'll be able to visit home once a month. After that, I'll come home every weekend."

"Really?" Mom asks incredulously.

"Yes, that's the rule," Eda says, looking her directly in the eye.

"Your father will not be happy."

"But why not, Mom?" I ask. "I think it sounds like fun! Maybe I can become a soldier some day!"

***

Today, when Eda comes home from the military office, she hands Papa an official-looking paper and proudly says, "Well, Papa, it's a done deal! I'm in! I'll be staying on the base for six months and come home once a month."

Little does Papa know that Eda voluntarily joined the military. I can't even imagine a day without my Eda, but I know she will be happy and safe . . . and away from Mom, if even for a short while.

***

I'm a high school student now, and with Eda gone to the military and Ed graduating from high school, I feel so grown up! But this bubble soon bursts. Almost everyone in my class is at least a year older than me, with some as many as three! The school law allows students to take the same school year for up to three years, so that makes me the youngest and the dumbest kid in the class.

I scoot around in my seat, trying to make myself comfortable. All the desks are lined up in rows of ten, with a total of thirty students. To my left sits a girl named Yasmine, and to my right, two older girls. We all introduce ourselves and, just like that, Yasmine—who likes to be called "Yassi"—and I become friends. She and I both agree the older girls are weird and should be in the university by now. All they ever talk about is boys!

Before long, a teacher comes into our classroom. "Hello, everyone. My name is Miss Moty. I am the art teacher. I have an announcement, so listen carefully. Our school has been selected to put on a show for Shah Bano's birthday celebration. There will be very important people here to honor our queen, such as the mayor, the superintendent, and many more. The program will be held on Mother's Day in Pahlavi Auditorium, which holds two hundred people." Miss Moty looks from face to face. "I need a few talented singers and someone who can put together a play."

All the students are quiet.

Miss Moty prods, "Anyone?"

In a flash, I raise my hand.

"What can you do?" Miss Moty asks me.

"Ma'am, I think I can create a play."

"You think?"

"Yes, ma'am."

"All right, tomorrow there will be an audition. Come to my classroom and we'll decide."

After she leaves, I wonder what I've gotten myself into. *Why did I raise my hand? What am I gonna do now? Oh, boy.*

***

As the day passes by, I come up with a plan. I think I can do this! I need two people: one to play the mom and one to play the angel. And we'll need a doll for the baby. I stage the story in my mind. The more I think about it, the better it gets.

I approach my new friend, Yassi, and my cousin Irene. "Hey, girls. Do you want to be in the play with me?" I ask.

"I'd love to!" Irene answers.

Yassi nods her head eagerly as well.

"Hooray!" I respond. "I'll tell you the story, and tomorrow we'll audition. If Miss Moty likes it, we'll need to start practicing since we only have two weeks until the performance."

After school, I tell Mom about the play. She asks, "Is that part of school? Play? Huh, instead of teaching you important things, they concentrate on play?"

I keep quiet, but I also keep rehearsing the play in my mind . . . and I love it!

What Success Feels Like

WE ALL RUSH TO Miss Moty's room to audition. Before we enter, I say, "I'll do the talking." Yassi and Irene trail behind me as we make our way into the class. Other girls are ahead of us, so we wait. Some of them sing for Miss Moty, while others act out a play.

Soon, Miss Moty points to us. "Come closer, girls."

"Hello, Miss Moty," we all say, inching our way toward her.

"So, what do you have for me?" she asks.

"Here, ma'am. I have the story," and I explain my idea for our play.

"That sounds good. What about costumes?"

"Miss Moty," I say, "I have my gymnastics leotard, but I need a pair of black tights and a black cape. The angel needs a dress with wings, and the mother needs a dress, too, and a doll for the baby. But don't worry, Irene's mom is a seamstress. I'm sure she can help us."

"Have you thought about music?" Miss Moty asks.

"Yes, ma'am. I'll ask my older brother to make it for me. I think I'd like to use 'Eclipse' by Pink Floyd."

"Well, it looks like you've thought of everything! The play is yours. I trust you," she says with a smile.

The three of us cheer.

"Wait a minute," Miss Moty adds. "You ladies are on your own now. You will need this special pass for class so you can practice."

"Thank you, Miss Moty!" I say with surprise.

Filing out of her room, we can hardly hold in our excitement. "We got it, girls!" I cheer, hugging Yassi and Irene. Now we can start practicing!"

"Hey, this means we can skip classes?" Yassi asks.

"Yes! Isn't that awesome?" I reply.

***

Day after day, we practice and get better. Even our costumes are coming together, thanks to Auntie Lydia. Not only is she making our costumes, she even offered to buy me my black tights!

I know Miss Moty is coming tomorrow to watch our rehearsal, and we still need our music, so I go to my brother. "Um, Ed, can you please record some music for my play?"

"No, I don't care about your stupid play."

"Ed, please. I need it for tomorrow."

"I don't care," he repeats. "Go do it yourself."

"Ed, please! I don't know how!"

"Oh, God. You won't leave me alone, will you?" Ed goes to our cassette player and says, "Give me an empty cassette tape."

I try to find one.

He spits out, "Never mind. I got it. What song do you want?"

"'Eclipse.'"

"Pink Floyd?"

"Yes, I think it would be great!"

"Huh, what a choice," he snickers. "I didn't know you had such taste in music, you ding-dong."

I smile. "Well, I do."

Ed keeps his word and copies the song for me. We're all set!

***

I'm in front of the school when Irene and Yassi arrive at seven-thirty in the morning. "Let's go, girls. Hurry up! We need to get ready before Miss Moty comes."

Irene says, "Okay, I've got all of our costumes."

We head quickly to the art room to wait for Miss Moty. We just goof around, teasing and poking each other, when she walks in.

"Good morning, Miss Moty!" we chorus.

"Good morning! Are you girls ready?"

"Yes, ma'am."

"Then let's go!"

Irene, Yassi, and I give each other questioning looks.

"Where are we going?" I ask.

"Oh, I forgot to tell you. We're going to rehearse at the auditorium where you will be performing."

"We are?" I ask, with eyes open wide.

"Yes, ma'am!"

We all shrug and smile at each other.

We pack our things, along with the tape player, and walk. It's even more fun because we're walking away from school during school hours, when everyone else is sitting in their classrooms.

I elbow Yassi and Irene and giggle. "You girls should thank me since I got you out of school."

"Here, this way," Miss Moty says, walking in front of us. We turn toward the alley and then up the tall steps and into the building. Miss Moty holds the door open for us, and what we see is more than we could ever have imagined.

"Whoa, look at the seats!" Yassi says.

"Look at the stage! It's huge!" I add.

"Hurry up, girls. It's time to get ready!" Miss Moty nudges.

We walk backstage, where I change into my leotard and tights, quickly wrap my cape around my shoulders, and tie my ponytail up high. Yassi's ready, but Irene struggles with her angel wings.

"Do you need help?" I ask.

"Yes, please."

I call for Yassi's help, and together we attach Irene's wings.

"Set the music," Miss Moty tells me.

"Yes, ma'am."

We make our way onto the stage. It's dark until Miss Moty turns the stage lights on. As I position myself, I notice some people in the seats. *I guess we have an audience?*

"Are you ready?" Miss Moty asks.

"Yes, ma'am." The music begins and I show off my moves, as do Yassi and Irene.

At the end, Miss Moty praises, "Good job!" Then she comes to me and adds, "How did you learn to dance like this, Ariana?"

"I learned the moves in my gymnastics class. I love to dance!"

"Well, you sure impressed the superintendent and me. Well done!"

I feel so good inside! I run to Irene and Yassi. "Let's pack up our stuff, girls. We have to go back to school. Just think, next Friday is *the day*." Friday can't come fast enough!

***

I'm sure Mom knows this program is for school.

"Mom, do you think you can come watch my program?" I ask with doubt.

"Of course not. Are you out of your mind? I have to cook."

"I didn't think so," I mutter to myself, and leave the house.

***

I meet up with Yassi and Irene at the bus stop near Irene's house. We walk, talk, giggle, and talk and giggle some more.

I ask, "Are your families coming to watch?"

"Of course," Yassi and Irene reply.

"Isn't yours?" Yassi asks.

Irene jumps in. "Um, her mom is a little strange," tapping me on my shoulder.

"Let's cross the street!" I say, changing the subject.

With the auditorium before us, I say, "Here we are, girls. Today is the day! Dah-dah-da-dah!"

As we make our way inside, we find it's very busy with other students, teachers, and staff. We help each other into our costumes and go through the things we don't want to forget.

"Remember to stay calm and don't be nervous," I chide.

Irene adds, "We mustn't forget to hold each other's hands when we curtsy."

"And don't make me drop my doll," Yassi warns.

Meanwhile, we can hear the audience growing louder as more arrive.

"Do I look pretty?" Irene asks Yassi and me, as she applies more dark-pink blush to her cheeks.

"Yes, Irene. You are very pretty," I say.

Miss Moty comes over our way. "All right girls, take a deep breath. It's your turn. Remember, just like rehearsal." She pats me on my shoulder, declaring, "You'll do great!", then steps back.

The red velvet curtain opens up to each side as "Eclipse" plays from the speakers. I can do this! I step up, fix my cape, and take a few big steps out onto the stage. The spotlight chases every move I make, as I begin my naughty, evil dance. I jump high with my feet wide apart, just like a Russian gymnast, then I cover my face with my black cape and land back down on the stage. Back and forth, I present myself by dragging my feet with authority; swaying my body from side to side. I fall to the ground, roll around, and jump back up again, opening my arms to reveal my vicious face, with my cape flowing behind me.

Yassi stands nearby, rocking her baby. I try to take the baby away from her, until Irene, the angel, appears. A battle ensues; evil tries to win, but the angel ends up saving the baby. She pushes my evil away. I jump one more time, I split, and cover my face with my cape. The music stops. My heart is pounding. I hear the audience, all 200 of them. Applauding; some even whistling. I look up, and with one graceful move, I stand. *Oh my God, I did it!*

Irene and Yassi come to me. The three of us hold each other's hands and curtsy to the audience. I smile like I've never smiled before and I think, *This is what success must feel like.*

As I leave the stage with pride, in my heart I still worry. If I get home late or if Mom notices my stage makeup, how will she react? It's a constant battle inside me that never surrenders.

1975–1977
Daffodils

THE FIRST YEAR OF EDA'S military service ended. She now comes home every day. Meanwhile, she's working in a veterans hospital, where she'll serve for the next year until the end of her term. Every time I see Eda in her khaki uniform, with her lavender bandana and name tag upon her chest, I think how beautiful she is. Not only is she beautiful, she is a serious soldier who can shoot a gun with no mistakes. She even took first place in her ranking! She's for real, you know?

Eda just got home. While she changes into her house clothes, I help Mom set the table. I hear the doorbell.

"Are we expecting someone?" I ask and walk to the door. "Oh, hi, Auntie Janet." My auntie is married to Papa's brother, Uncle Miktar. And since Mom doesn't have any sisters, we call all of my uncles' wives "auntie."

"Mom, it's Auntie Janet," I announce, noticing a basket full of daffodils in her hand. "What's this, Auntie?"

She smiles, and with a sweet, friendly motion, pushes me away, saying, "It's not for you, girl."

"It must be from some guy, Auntie. I'm sure it's for Eda!"

Auntie sits at the table, keeping the bouquet in front of her.

"The flowers are so beautiful," I say, staring at the long-stemmed yellow daffodils. "There must be a hundred!"

Auntie says, "I know, that's right. Now go get your sister."

Before I run to the bedroom to let Eda know, I inhale the sweet aroma.

"Eda, Eda, come! Someone sent you flowers!"

"What? What flowers? For me?" Eda questions.

Sitting beside Mom, Auntie Janet calls, "Come here, Eda."

While Eda greets Auntie, I go and sit on the floor near the kerosene heater. Through the kitchen window, I see snowflakes falling. From this corner of the dining room, I also see Eda rubbing her hands together under the table. I don't want to miss a thing!

"Hello, Eda. I have a special delivery," Auntie says, unable to contain herself.

Eda looks puzzled.

"There's this young man who is a friend of our family. He has seen you at some gatherings and is very interested in meeting you."

Eda bashfully looks at Mom. "I don't know what to say. I think I know who you're talking about."

"Well, there is a dinner coming up. He's wondering if he might have the honor to take you as his date."

Mom jumps in. "Janet, who is he? What kind of job does he have? How old is he? And what's his name? Jacob is not going to be happy if we don't know anything about this boy. Our daughter didn't grow up under a tree."

"Liz, don't make such a fuss about it. If he wasn't a decent guy, would I even come to ask?" She gives her sister-in-law a comforting look. "His name is Shant. He's very good-looking, with piercing blue eyes. He is a very successful hairdresser, and I've known him and his family forever. Shant's ready for a commitment, and, if Eda likes him, he will pamper and treat her like a princess. So, what do you say, Eda?"

Eda, who has been quiet all this time, calmly replies, "Well, if it's all right with Mom and Papa, I'd like to meet him, too."

"That sounds great! I'll let him know." Auntie Janet gives Eda an approving hug and leaves.

"Well, Eda, you have to know there are rules and boundaries," Mom explains. "If you end up liking him after you meet, you should get married very soon."

"Yes, Mom. I know."

Ed shows up in the middle of the conversation, sees the flowers, and blurts out, "Is this from a guy for you, Eda?"

"Yes," I say. "He wants to marry her." I am beaming.

"Who is this *esh* who wants to marry *you*, Eda?" he guffaws.

"Oh, shut up, Ed," we all say in unison.

***

Soon after the flower delivery, Eda and Shant begin dating. He is very trendy, good-looking, and everyone likes him. He always brings presents, chocolates, or flowers for Eda and our family. Sometimes, he even takes us out for dinner! But when he and Eda go on a date and he has to drop her off before midnight, Eda's curfew, he gets upset.

Eda tells me, "Every time I go out with Shant, I worry sick. It's unbelievable to him that our parents are so strict; that I have a midnight curfew. We can only see each other once a week for a couple of hours. He likes to dance, so he takes me to the disco, but before we go onto the dance floor, we have to leave. I'm so ready to get out of this house! I can't wait to be married!"

Sometimes if Eda gets home past her curfew, I can't sleep. Mom keeps cursing, and her ultimatums scare me. I keep going to the window to see if Eda is coming and I tell myself she'll be home any minute. I pray, *Dear Lord, please make Mom fall asleep so she won't notice if Eda comes home late. Please, dear Lord.*

A few times, as soon as I hear Shant's car getting closer, I tiptoe to the door and carefully unlock it, so when Eda comes in, the key in the door from the outside won't make noise. But it happened, more often than not, that Eda would come in just five minutes past curfew.

Mom's uncontrolled rage and ridicule were always there to ruin Eda's evening. Mom was never short on cursing or even slapping her.

With her head down in defeat, Eda would retreat to her bedroom and brush away the pain in her soul with a ray of hope for tomorrow.

***

After many arguments between Eda and Mom, the brief dating period is over. Eda announced today that Shant has asked her to marry him.

"Well, what did you say, Eda? Did you say yes? Did you?" I was about to come out of my skin.

"Well, of course I said yes."

"Yay!"

"Shut up," Mom says to me. "It's none of your business." Turning to Eda, she asks rudely, "So when are his parents coming to ask permission from your father and me? What the hell do they think? That just like that, you two can get married?"

"Wait, Mom. His parents want to come and ask permission whenever it is convenient for you and Papa."

"Well, I'll have to speak with your father."

"When is Papa coming home?" Eda asks.

"Maybe tomorrow. I don't know."

Papa comes home later than Mom anticipated. Once he showered and smoked his cigarette, Mom brings him some dates and a cup of tea.

"Tell me. What's new?" Papa asks.

"Come here, Eda," Mom says.

Eda comes and sits across the table. She bends her head down and holds her hands under the table. I know she's rubbing them together.

Sitting next to Papa, I dangle my feet and twist the bottom of my colorful sweater around my finger. I can't wait to see Papa's face when he hears the news!

Mom gazes at me from behind her thick eyeglasses, making her look even more scary. "You nosy little brat. Don't you say a word."

I slide down in my seat and hang my head. Ed joins us from the other room, where he was drawing a floor plan for his pre-architecture class.

"When's the wedding, Eda?" Ed asks mischievously.

Papa looks at Eda and attempts to control his emotions. "He finally asked you to marry him?"

"Yes, Papa. If it's all right, his family can come and visit you and Mom."

"Liz, when is a good day?" Papa asks.

Their conversation rattles on for some time, and finally, a date is agreed upon.

***

Eda and I help Mom clean the house, arranging and rearranging the furniture. She's even put out her fine china. The house sparkles and smells divine with Mom's cooking. She has put a lot of effort into showing off her talent. The kitchen table, oven, and stove are filled with scrumptious food and appetizers such as stuffed grape leaves (Armenian *dolma*), green bean casserole, Persian dill rice, fried shrimp, and fish.

Once everything is set up, we all change into our best clothes. Eda wears a soft pink blouse and a gray skirt with a touch of makeup. I have on a red and navy pleated skirt with a white blouse. Mom can't decide between several dresses laid out on her bed.

"Ariana, Josh, come in here," Mom calls.

"I wonder what she wants with us," Josh asks.

"I don't know. With Mom, there's no telling. Let's go."

Placing my hands on Josh's shoulders, I walk with him to Mom's bedroom. I'm nervous inside. "Yes, Mom," I say.

Mom grabs my ear with one hand and Josh's ear with the other. "Both of you listen to me carefully. If you misbehave, I will beat you in front of all the guests. Do you hear me? Is that clear?"

"Yes, Mom," I say with a shaky voice.

Josh just nods.

Soon, the doorbell rings. Shant, his parents, sisters, brother, and uncles arrive. Josh and I are on our best behavior.

"Please, please, come on in," Mom greets all the guests, directing them to the formal dining room. Josh and I stay out as Eda places a beautiful bouquet of flowers from Shant into a vase. She then serves tea to her future in-laws.

With some prelude, Shant's mother, Mrs. Karina, asks Papa and Mom, "Mr. Jacob and Mrs. Liz, as you know, we are here to ask for your daughter's hand in marriage. We assure you that our Shant will take good care of your daughter. If you permit, we can set a wedding date so this young couple might start their lives."

"Mrs. Karina and Mr. Kavork," Papa says very politely, "of course we agree to their marriage. As much as you want happiness for your son, we wish the same for our Eda. Therefore, they have our blessing." Papa stands up and goes to Eda and Shant, takes each of their hands, and puts them together. Everyone applauds and cheers, "To the future bride and groom!"

Josh and I stand outside the room, peeking and giggling.

Josh keeps asking, "What are they saying?"

"Shhh, be quiet!"

Shant stands up and takes a small red velveteen box out of his pocket. He slowly opens it, takes a beautiful ring out, and puts it on Eda's finger. I can't wait any longer! Taking a risk, I run to the edge of the dining room and slowly ease my way over to Eda. There I can get a good look at my sister's engagement ring. I hold Eda's hand in mine. My eyes are open wide and I grin from ear to ear.

"Oh my gosh! Look at this diamond. It's huge! Look, Josh!" I call my brother to join my excitement. We both inspect Eda's sparkly ring. It's a solitaire diamond set on a platinum band. It looks so pretty on Eda's delicate hand. Shant is just about to kiss Eda when she pulls back. "Oh, thank you! It's so pretty!" she says, looking down at her new engagement ring.

"Cheers to our bride and groom!" Papa announces.

With her jaw clenched, Mom glares at me—a look that tells me I will pay for intruding—as she heads to the kitchen for a bottle of brand new cognac and a box of chocolates to serve.

I notice Shant's face. He looks disappointed. I think he's upset that Eda didn't let him kiss her. He must not know that in my house, we're not allowed to do things like that. Papa doesn't believe touching or hugging, much less kissing, anyone but your siblings is acceptable.

As everyone takes a shot of cognac and a piece of chocolate, Mrs. Karina suggests setting a wedding date. After going back and forth, the date is set: October eighteenth.

I run to my beautiful Eda and we embrace her new beginning; just like a daffodil, a symbol of new life.

Something Borrowed

I DON'T GET TO SEE Eda that much anymore. She's either working at the hospital or shopping with Mom for bridal furniture, but I'm still excited. Eda and Shant will be married in just a few months!

And since I'm going to be a bridesmaid, I get to wear a long, white dress, almost identical to my sister's. How cool is that? Our Armenian traditions are fun—sometimes.

Mom takes me to look for a dress. I'm almost fourteen, and still I have no say. After we've been shopping for several hours, Mom chooses a dress with a flowy scarf that hangs over my shoulders. I think it's pretty.

The clerk, a young man with bushy dark hair, brings me the dress to try on. "You can change over there." He points at the black curtain hanging from the ceiling.

With hesitation, I go behind the curtain and change.

"Are you done?" Mom asks in a loud voice.

"Yes," and I rush out before she gets mad.

The clerk says, "That looks really nice on her."

"Yes, that is a pretty dress, but it looks uneven in the mid-section," Mom says.

"Come closer, young lady," calls the clerk.

Reluctantly, I take a few steps and stand in front of him with my back to Mom. There's something about him I just don't like. He kneels and puts his hands under my long dress on my thighs and pretends he is smoothing the lining of the dress. I hate his touch and try to pull away from him. But Mom, behind me, holds onto my shoulders and says, "She is almost fourteen, yet she can't stand still."

The man, who is still smoothing my dress, looks at me with a nasty smile, then removes his hands from underneath my dress. I am disgusted, and I wish Mom would hurry up, so we can leave. *Why didn't Mom stop the man? Didn't she notice his nasty smile?*

***

When we get home, I show it off to Ed and Eda.

"It looks pretty, Ariana. I like it!" Eda says.

Ed makes fun of me. "You better make sure you keep that dress covering your legs all the way to your toes so you won't scare anyone with your hairy legs. People will think you are a monkey in a white dress!"

"*Esh!*" I leave the room crying.

"What's wrong with you, Ed? Leave her alone!" Eda scolds.

"Well, look at her legs! They're covered in hair!"

"Ed, be quiet! Mom won't allow her to shave her legs. Just stop!"

***

After many days of shopping, our formal dining room and the corner of our bedroom are filled with brand new bedding, small household items, and kitchen tools—all for Eda. Every time Mom or Eda comes home from shopping, the stacks get bigger and taller. Of course, every chance Mom gets, she flaunts Eda's trove to my aunt and even neighbors.

This evening, Eda announces she has a wedding gown. "Hurray! Where is it?"

Mom stares at me. "How many times do I have to tell you that this is none of your business!"

"Sorry, Mom." I try to keep my happiness inside, but can't wait to see Eda's gown!

When Mom is done scolding me, she turns to Eda. "What are you talking about? You already bought the dress?"

"Well, Shant's older sister knows this lady who recently got married, and she is allowing me to borrow it," Eda replies nonchalantly. "I tried on the dress, and Shant, his sisters, and mom liked it."

"Does it fit you?"

"It's a little loose on my chest and the sleeves are kind of long, but it doesn't matter," Eda says.

"How does it look?" Mom asks.

"It's a simple chiffon dress with a train."

"What about your headpiece?"

"That's also borrowed from someone else," Eda says.

"What does it look like?"

"It's a big white hat with a floppy brim and a short veil of tulle, just long enough to cover my face."

"Eda, you should have your own gown," Mom criticizes. "Are you crazy?"

"Mom, please. It doesn't matter to me."

Watching and listening to Eda, I worry that she is overwhelmed with her wedding plans.

"Eda, will I get to see your gown?"

"No, Ariana. Not until my wedding day."

"That stinks!" Knowing in our Armenian tradition the groom keeps the wedding dress until the day of the wedding, I lose hope.

I see how everything is happening so fast for my sister, and sometimes I see frustration in her, especially when she can't sleep at night.

When we are alone, I ask, "Eda, do you love him?"

She turns to me, pauses, and taking a deep breath, says, "Why do you ask? You're too young to think of this. He's a nice man and I love him. He gets jealous sometimes and I feel pressured, but I can deal with that. It's better than putting up with Mom." She then becomes quiet, and I say no more.

Eda's Gown

TODAY, MY CHILDISH HAPPINESS is beyond belief! I put on my dress and pin my long hair away from my face. Ed, Josh, and Papa are dressed in their brand new black suits and white button-down shirts with black neckties, while Mom wears her new maroon, beaded gown.

Ed helps Mom set up the drinks and Papa, trying not to show his excitement, double-checks everything.

Eda has gone to the hair salon, where Shant's brother fixes her hair, and comes home with a much fuller and curlier hairstyle. Her eyes are lined with a brush of light brown shadow, making her eyes look even more striking. Bronze blush accents her distinguished cheekbones, and a touch of lipstick outlines her lips.

"Eda, you look so beautiful!"

She looks at me and sighs.

"Are you all right, Eda?"

"I don't know. I don't look like myself." She grabs a napkin, folds it in half, and dabs at her lips. With the tip of her pinkie, she blends the remaining lipstick, then produces a rat-tailed comb and calms some of the curls.

"Huh, you look even prettier now, Eda!"

***

A little while later, the doorbell rings.

"They're here! They're here!" Josh and I yell and run to answer it.

"Stay away and behave!" Mom orders, pointing her forefinger menacingly.

She opens the door to the three-man folk band and their instruments: an accordion, a flute, and a *daira*. The band begins with the man and his big bulky accordion hanging from his shoulders in front of him. As he opens and closes the instrument, he presses on different buttons and keys, swaying side to side to the music. The man with the flute holds it in front of himself, moving it up and down, tapping his fingers on the holes, blowing into it. The person with the *daira* holds the big barrel covered with sheepskin under his arm, and, with his other hand, he dances his fingers and palms, creating different notes. The music is perfect, with all three singing the wedding songs.

Behind them come Shant, his parents, sisters, brother, and his brother's wife, along with the best man. They carry big bouquets of flowers, baskets of presents, chocolates, and, best of all, Eda's wedding gown.

The two families congratulate each other as drinks are served and music plays. The women take the wedding gown to the bedroom to help Eda get ready and the men have a drink and carry on. Josh and I go outside to the alley, where we see Shant's car parked all decked out with a blanket of white carnations.

I hear the music get louder, so we run inside.

There is Eda. She looks so elegant, all dressed in white. The short veil hanging from her borrowed hat covers her face. She walks through the crowd. Shant, all dressed up in a black suit, holds a small bouquet of white orchids. He walks toward Eda and hands her the flowers, before they walk toward Papa. The music stops, and all is quiet.

Papa looks to Eda and Shant. "My children, I wish you happiness and love. Respect one another and have faith. You have God's blessing, and mine, too."

Papa's about to cry as he places Eda's hand into Shant's. Quickly, he picks up his glass of cognac, clears his throat, and toasts, "To our bride and groom! Let's take this to the priest now before we all get drunk!"

Everyone cheers as Eda and Shant make their way to the door.

Keeping with Armenian tradition, Ed blocks the door with his hands. "Not so fast," Ed announces.

Shant steps up. "Okay, how can I get your permission, young man?"

"Well, let's see. I have been guardian to my sister for a long time, and I have kept her safe for you. What do you have to offer?"

Shant reaches in his pocket and takes out a large gold coin. "Would this be sufficient for the protection which you have provided?"

Ed takes the coin, checks it out, and says, "Hmmm. I think so."

Everyone applauds as Ed lets them pass by. The bride and groom rush to the waiting car, while neighbors, trying to get a glimpse of Eda, cheer and toss sugared almonds at them.

As we enter the church, the seats begin to fill quickly. Nina and I stand behind Eda to keep an eye on her train; to keep it smooth and neat.

The piano plays. With Shant on one side of Eda and the best man on the other, they start walking slowly toward the altar where the priest stands. He holds the Holy Bible wrapped in a white handkerchief in one hand and a big silver cross in the other. My beautiful Eda looks like a swan, graceful and calm.

The ceremony begins with the priest raising his big silver cross and reciting a verse from the Bible, and the two women and three men in the choir join in their chorus. The bride and groom face each other; the best man holds a cross over their heads.

It's now time to exchange the rings. The best man quickly reaches to the side pocket of his suit, takes the rings out, and holds them in front of the priest to be blessed. Eda and Shant hold each other's hands. The guests are quiet; the choir has stopped.

The priest reads, "Shant, will you receive Eda as your wife? Do you pledge to her your love, faith, and tenderness, and cherish her with a husband's loyalty and devotion?"

"I do," Shant says.

"Now, Eda, will you receive Shant as your husband? Do you pledge to him your love, faith, and tenderness, and cherish him with a wife's loyalty and devotion?"

Eda softly says, "I do."

"I now pronounce you husband and wife."

The ceremony ends with the best man, the bride, and the groom drinking wine from one glass. Then Shant and Eda turn to each other, and he pulls back her veil. Everyone applauds.

They walk toward the door as the church bell rings. Right when it's opened, it starts to rain. As the raindrops tickle my upturned face, I smile, knowing it is a sign of good luck.

Everyone rushes to their cars. Nina and I get to ride with Eda and Shant to the reception hall. Shant holds Eda's hand and he kisses her lips.

Bashfully, Eda says, "Okay, you're messing up my makeup."

Nina and I look at each other and giggle.

Arriving at the reception hall, we hear the music playing from the parking lot. As we make our way inside, all the guests welcome the bride and groom with applause and the throwing of sweets and flowers. The happy couple takes to the dance floor as a soft waltz begins. Everyone sits down, admiring the bride and the groom, but mostly, my beautiful Eda. As they dance, from time to time, Eda smiles.

The celebration goes on for hours, until it's time to say farewell. Eda now stands with her husband, saying goodbye to the guests, Papa, Mom, Ed, Josh, and finally me.

Papa says, "My daughter, respect your husband. And son, take good care of my daughter."

Mom hugs Eda and cries a little. I'm stunned. She has never done this, ever.

Ed taps on Shant's shoulder. "My man, don't mess with my sister." They exchange a knowing look, an unspoken promise.

Josh wraps himself around Eda's legs and won't let go. "Eda, I want you to come with us," he pleads.

Eda replies, "I will come visit you. I promise!"

Mom pulls Josh away.

I just realized Eda won't be coming home with us. I hug her and try so hard not to cry.

"Shhh, Ariana. I'll come to see you guys very soon. Don't be sad," Eda says as she wipes away my tears.

I let go, and we leave for home. Once we arrive, I change, wash up, and go to bed after a long day. Eda's side of the bed is empty. I bury my face in her pillow and cry myself to sleep.

Another Rampage

ED USUALLY HANGS OUT with Matthew during the day and they end up at our house for lunch. Matthew is his friend of several years; a polite, lovable young man, very tall and buff. While I'm setting the kitchen table for lunch, Mom sautés diced onions. I slice the fresh Barbary, my favorite bread, and place it on the table with salt and pepper shakers, along with angelica powder, the secret herb for chili. Ed, Matthew, Josh, and I wait impatiently until Mom brings a big serving bowl of delicious chili.

During the meal, Matthew starts a conversation about a road trip to the beach, asking Ed, "Do you think you'll be able to go with us?"

Mom stops dead in her tracks. "What are you talking about, Matthew? Where are you going?"

Matthew replies, "Auntie, we have family friends who live at the beach and we can stay in their house."

"Are you going to drive?" Mom asks.

"Don't worry, Auntie. My other friends, who are also going, are older than Ed and me. My friend Ali will be driving, and he is a good driver."

"First, I have to talk to your parents. Then I'll decide."

Once Matthew has left, Mom makes it clear she is not happy about the trip; keeps talking to herself, mumbling, "Huh, now he decides to go on a road trip without even asking me first!"

I keep quiet as I wash the dishes. I can anticipate when Mom is about to lose it.

"Ed, come here!" Mom demands.

Walking out of his bedroom, Ed says, "Yes, Mom? What is it?"

"Where do you think you're going? Not even telling me?"

"Mom, I was going to tell you, and Papa, too. Matthew just came up with the idea. To tell you the truth, it was his mom's idea. Plus, it's not until next week."

"Oh, really? You think I'll let you go? Over my dead body!"

I'm still in the kitchen and Josh is playing with his toy. We look at each other, both scared. I know this fight is going to be a bad one.

"Josh, don't move. Stay right here, away from Mom," I order him, hoping this will keep him safe.

I walk slowly toward the dining room where Mom and Ed are arguing. Now Ed, being older and strong, is not holding back. Their voices are getting louder.

"You can't tell me what to do anymore. I'm old enough to have friends and do things."

"Shut up, you piece of shit! You are nobody! You are nothing!"

"Mom, don't raise your voice at me. You can't scare me anymore."

"Really? Now you tell me what to do? You jerk!" And she throws her wooden spatula at Ed. I'm standing near the kitchen door in a panic. *How can I stop this?*

Ed approaches Mom. As he gets closer, Mom slaps him, leaving her finger marks on his face.

"Mom, stop it!" He grabs both of Mom's hands. "I'm not a five-year-old boy anymore."

Mom is furious. She looks like she is ready to kill. Her hands are still being pushed back by Ed, but she manages to knee him in his private area. "You piece of shit!" Mom curses as Ed falls to his knees and bends over in pain. "I hope you die a painful death!"

As Mom keeps cursing, she kicks Ed in his back. He gets up slowly, trying so hard to control his anger, but Mom, on the other hand, is not. She charges at Ed and slaps him again and again and calls him a faggot.

"Mom, stop it! How many times have I told you not to call me names?" Ed shouts.

I can't take it anymore. I get closer to Mom to try and calm her down. Ed flees the house, slamming the door. The narrow glass window breaks. Shattered glass flies everywhere. Even the door looks broken.

As she is about to go after Ed, I beg, "Mom, please leave him alone."

She turns around, teeth clenched and fists tightened, and takes angry steps toward me. I panic. At the same time, I see Josh hiding under the kitchen table. With my hand, I tell him to stay. Mom is in my face. I hold my elbow up to protect myself. She grabs my wrist with her strong hand and, with one quick motion, twists it to my back, squeezing my arm. She slaps me with all her might.

"Mom, please."

"You slut! You bitch! Why can't you just die and burn in hell?"

I see she is about to slap me again, so I turn my face. Her hand finds its target on my cheek and forces my head to bash into the wall behind me. I crumble.

She screams, "Whore! You try to defend that loser?"

"No, Mom!"

She has picked up a kitchen chair. I flash back to when she broke the chair on Ed's back. In a quick move, I crawl to the other side of the room and decide to run for my life. There's no one to save me, and she *will* kill me this time.

Mom is right behind me. "You whore! If you leave this house, I'm gonna kill you!"

I keep running and praying, *Please, God, help me.* I flee down the alley and cross the road to my Uncle Ted's house. I yell, "Uncle Ted! Auntie Emma, please open the door!" I hear Mom behind me screaming and cursing nasty words. I pound on the door. "Please, please open the door!"

Auntie Emma opens the door and I rush in. "What's going on?" Auntie Emma worriedly asks.

All that comes out is, "It's Mom!"

Mom storms in after me, hatred and venom spewing from her lips.

Auntie Emma tries to make sense of it all. "Liz, wait. What's going on?"

Mom shouts and calls me horrible names. My grandma, my cousins, and Uncle Ted stare with wide eyes and mouths agape. I try to shelter myself behind Uncle Ted, but Mom grabs my half-undone ponytail. In one swift move, she wraps my hair around her hand and pulls me to the ground. Mercilessly, she drags me across the carpet as I hold my head. I feel like my scalp is about to rip apart. Uncle Ted grabs Mom's arm, but she jerks away and spits on him.

"Leave me alone!" she screams. "I have to kill her!"

Suddenly, someone from behind grabs Mom and pushes her away with great force. Free, I lie there numb, motionless. This is when I notice the person who stopped Mom was Matthew's brother, who happened to be passing by the house. He must have noticed the commotion since the entry door was ajar.

Auntie Emma holds my body, trying to help me stand up. It is difficult for me to breathe. She takes me to her bedroom, sits me on the bed, and gets me a glass of water. My hands are trembling so hard Auntie Emma has to hold the glass for me. My teeth tap the glass. My head is so full of pain I can't even touch it. I sob uncontrollably.

"Don't cry, my darling," Auntie Emma says, pulling me to her chest, caressing my shoulder. "My darling, it's okay. You know your mom is a nervous person. She can't control her anger."

I lift my head and look at my auntie with such sadness it penetrates my soul. "Auntie Emma, how is it that everyone says 'it's okay'? It's 'okay' for Mom to hurt me? To hurt Ed and Eda?"

It seems like everyone is afraid of her. If Papa raises his voice, she cries, becomes breathless and faints. It makes Papa pity her. This is how, all these years, she has gotten away with hurting us. No one, not even Papa, notices that it's all an act.

What have I done that is so bad to deserve a punishment like this? What have I done except be her child? And that, I did not choose.

A Young Life Lost

IT TOOK A WHILE FOR me to mentally recover, or at least pretend I had forgotten, Mom's rampage. Since Ed has left, and with Papa always gone, I keep my distance from her, yet try to protect little Josh. He especially loves it when I sing cartoon songs to him.

As I help Mom wash vegetables, she asks me, "Where do you think your brother might be?"

"I don't know, Mom."

"I wonder if he went on that trip with Matthew." She looks directly at me. "You two always cover for each other. Now you're telling me you don't know anything?"

Crossing my fingers behind my back, I say, "I swear to you, Mom. I'm telling the truth."

"It's been ten days since he left the house—not that I care. My concern is for your father. When he comes home and your brother isn't here, he'll get really upset."

I know she wants me to tell her where Ed is staying. Ha! Wishful thinking.

***

Ed is not mentioned again for several days, until Papa comes home. His last trip has been a long one. He's filthy and his clothes are covered in white salt.

"Papa, you look like you really need a bath!"

"Of course, *Baless*. Don't touch my clothes."

"They look stiff."

Papa chuckles. "Sure they are. Let me take a shower and get cleaned up."

I walk to the kitchen to make a cup of tea for Papa, and ask Mom, "Do you know Papa is home?"

She shrugs and carelessly says, "What do you want me to do?"

I avert my eyes from her glare and continue preparing Papa's tea. He loves it when his tea is waiting for him.

After cleaning up, Papa relaxes and takes a sip of tea, then hollers, "Hi, Liz! I'm home."

Mom sarcastically replies, "Welcome home."

"Where's Ed, Ariana?" he asks.

Since Mom is in the kitchen, preparing deep-fried chicken and mashed potatoes, I whisper, "Papa, he's been gone for nearly two weeks now. Mom hit him and called him names." I quickly change the subject as Mom enters the room.

She turns to me and says, "Come set the table for dinner and make some salad."

I head to the kitchen, with Josh right behind me, and do as Mom asked.

"Aren't you hungry?" Mom asks Papa.

"Of course, I am," Papa answers, then walks to the kitchen and takes a seat. "My belly can't wait any longer." He smiles at me.

I return the smile, then sit down next to Josh. Slowly, I put my index finger to my lips, telling him to keep quiet and eat.

"Liz, where is Ed? How come he's not coming to sit with us at the dinner table?"

"I don't know where he is."

"Should we wait for him to join us?"

"No, of course not," she answers, with another tirade written all over her face. "Can you just not talk about him? He has darkened my life. Why can't you understand this?" Mom's voice gets louder; her eyes have gone pitch-black.

I hold Josh's tiny cold hand in mine under the table to comfort him.

"All right, Liz. Calm down. Let's enjoy our dinner."

"Enjoy my dinner? Do you have any idea what I have to put up with? After I asked him one question about a trip Matthew was suggesting, that jerk son of yours made a scene, telling me, 'I'll go wherever I want, with whomever I want.'" Mom's voice goes up an octave. "He shouted at me, broke my crystal vase, and kicked the door down."

In the middle of her twisting the truth and telling her side of the story, Ed walks in. The room goes quiet as Ed roars, "Matthew's dead!" He falls to his knees with his hands on his head, hunkering down.

I don't understand and turn to Papa and Mom for answers. "What?" I ask in disbelief. "Matthew? You mean your best friend, Matthew?"

"Lord have mercy!" Mom exclaims. "This can't be true!" And she disappears out the door.

I know she's running to Matthew's house, a block down the road, hoping to find out he's lying.

Papa grabs hold of Ed's shoulders. "Son, son, look at me! What are you saying?"

"Papa, my best friend is dead. Matthew is dead!"

I don't know how long Papa holds Ed to his chest; my brother's guttural cries tug at my heartstrings. Tears escape, cascading from my own eyes.

"Son, calm yourself. Tell me what you know."

Ed tries hard to pull himself together. "Papa, Matthew went on a trip with some friends. I was supposed to go with him, but I was upset and I didn't go. Supposedly, he had a car accident and was found dead at the scene. If I had gone with him, this wouldn't have happened! Papa, it's my fault!"

"No, son. Don't say that. Even if you were there, you couldn't have saved him. It was his time to go. There's nothing you could have done."

With determination, Ed says, "Papa, no matter what you say, I will never forgive myself for not being there for him. Why did he have to die? He was only seventeen years old! Papa, I think he was killed, and it wasn't an accident!"

The rest of the night and the following week are filled with sorrow. The entire neighborhood mourns for the young life lost.

***

On the day of the funeral, Ed goes to the morgue to say goodbye to his best friend. He is joined by Matthew's brother and father. Upon request, only close family can see his body at the morgue before it's transported. In the meantime, I have to stay home with Josh and my cousins, while everyone else goes to the church and cemetery.

Later in the evening, when everyone is home, I ask Ed, "So, how did Matthew really die? Can you tell me?"

"Ariana, I can tell you it was no accident; it was a cover-up."

"What are you talking about?"

He sighs, getting his thoughts under control. "Ariana, what I saw at the morgue was not the Matthew I knew."

Papa invites Ed to sit down, asking, "Ed, what are you talking about? Son, keep yourself calm. I know how hard it can be to lose a friend. Tell me what's on your mind."

Ed takes a deep breath, exhaling slowly, trying to regain control, and begins, "Papa, everyone knows this. From out of nowhere, some strange woman started a friendship with Matthew's mother not too long ago. Soon, she became like a family member and began staying in their house." Ed looks directly into Papa's eyes. "During this period, Matthew's mom has traveled overseas several times."

"So what, Ed?" Papa asks.

"How is it Matthew's mother can travel so frequently and get a visa so quickly? How do they afford it? And strangely enough, their next-door neighbor's uncle, who works for the government intelligence service, SAVAK, is the one who took Matthew on the trip."

Papa frowns, thinking hard, trying to put the puzzle pieces together. I'm all ears, also trying to understand.

"Papa, this is what half the neighborhood and I think happened. We think the SAVAK agent planned the vacation through his nephew so Matthew would go with them. Matthew did just like they planned. When they arrived at wherever the meeting place was, the agent tried to question Matthew about the strange woman. Knowing Matthew, as naive as he was, most likely, he couldn't have answered any of the agent's questions. Then they tortured him to get an answer, until he died. Papa, I saw his body at the morgue. His knuckles, every single one of them, were purple and misshapen. His jaw was broken. His scalp . . . his scalp was skinned." Ed breaks down.

I rush over to Ed, holding him, crying. I can't believe what I'm hearing.

"Papa, my poor helpless friend was innocent. He didn't die in the car accident. The car was found in a small ditch. The driver walked out with no scratches and the passenger has gone cuckoo."

We all cry together. It's the first time I've seen Papa cry. A few minutes later, he collects himself and says firmly, "Son, what you believe has to stay inside you. You should not talk about this to anyone."

I ask Ed, "But where is the woman?"

"She has vanished. She wasn't at the funeral."

"Son, if it's said Matthew died in a car accident, so it is. Do you understand me?"

"Yes, Papa," he says, wiping his tears with the back of his hand.

Many times after this, I find Ed crying in his sleep. I don't know if it is the grief over the loss of his best friend, the guilt of not being there to save Matthew, or fear.

Since Matthew's Death

THE MEMORY OF MATTHEW'S mysterious death slowly fades. Ed, of course, is still in mourning and will forever be. Our conversations with each other are always serious now, leaving me with strange, uneasy feelings. Sometimes we speak of Matthew, SAVAK, and the strange woman with the Eastern-European accent who vanished like a drop of water. Sometimes we cry, wondering if we will ever find closure. Since Matthew's death, everything seems different. I don't know if it's just me growing up or if it's life.

I have come to realize there is growing talk about politics and the Shah's dictatorship. I even hear people have been taken prisoner and are being tortured! This must be why Papa doesn't like the regime. Often, he murmurs and curses the government, always warning us to stay away from conversations about the Shah and his rules.

***

Today, one of my distant uncles, whom I've never met, comes to visit Papa. I've heard about him and have gone many times to visit his wife and children, never knowing where their father was. They live in a low-income neighborhood in a tiny house, consisting of a living room and one bedroom. Furniture is sparse, and they don't even own a refrigerator! His wife, Auntie Tamar, is a very kind woman and a great seamstress. This is how she supports their two daughters and son. They may have very little, but they are intelligent and have hearts of gold. During our visits, Auntie often cries on Mom's shoulder, sharing the difficulties she faces every day. To help support her desperate situation, Papa and Mom often give her money.

"You must be Ariana," Uncle Gus says, reaching out to shake my hand.

With dancing eyes, I reply, "So glad to meet you, Uncle Gus."

My uncle is a middle-aged man, short and skinny, with gray hair, pale skin, and red cheeks. I sit quietly amongst them, anxious to hear what he has to say. The mood in the room seems serious.

"How are you feeling, Gus? When did you get out?" asks Papa.

"I got out two weeks ago, and somehow I made it through alive."

I couldn't keep quiet anymore. "Uncle, where were you? Where did you get out from?"

"I was in the Shah's prison for the last fifteen years."

"Oh, no! Are you against the Shah? Are you part of the Left Party?"

"Yes," Uncle replies.

Papa tilts his head and asks me, "How do you know about the Left Party, Ariana?"

"I know a little bit. I've read a few books, but I didn't really understand much until lately; mostly since Matthew's death."

Papa pats my hand, saying, "I'm glad you're beginning to realize the truth about our country."

I ask Uncle, "Have you been tortured?"

"Of course, Ariana," he answers as a man who has endured much. "Numerous times. I've had my knuckles broken with the butt of a pistol, hot needles pushed underneath my fingernails, and even electrical shocks."

I don't want to listen, but I do. It's too reminiscent of Matthew's injuries.

Then Papa says, "Ariana, you can't talk about this conversation to anyone. No one is to be trusted. SAVAK is everywhere."

"Yes, but it won't last long. The Shah's days are numbered," Uncle Gus says.

Later that evening, Uncle Gus shakes hands with Mom and gives Josh and me a big hug.

"Let's go, Jacob."

"After you, brother. I'll walk you to the end of the neighborhood."

Collecting the teacups and cookies left from the afternoon tea, I reflect on what I now know to be true. The young people who had been executed weren't terrorists at all. They were in opposition to the Shah's dictatorship. What I didn't know was that this would be the first and last time I would see Uncle Gus, a brave man who was never broken. I would later find out he had to flee the country.

Papa returns with the afternoon newspaper rolled under his arm. He pulls it out and sits down to read.

"Ariana, what year was your brother born?"

"Which one, Papa? Ed or Josh?"

"I want Ed's date of birth." Papa flattens out the newspaper, holding it down with both hands, his arms stiff, staring at it, motionless.

"1957, Papa. Why?"

That's when I see it. The news headline reads: ALL MEN BORN BETWEEN JANUARY OF 1950 AND AUGUST OF 1957 WILL BE CALLED TO DUTY. Ed's birthday is September first.

Papa exhales and hangs his head as the weight from his shoulders is released. "Thank God."

"That's great, Papa! I can't wait to give Ed the good news!"

"I am still worried for him. This is the best time for Ed to leave the country."

"Why are you still worried, Papa?"

"I don't know what the future will hold for him if he stays here, *Baless.*"

Shortly thereafter, Ed leaves for England. Even though my brother and I have had many arguments, we've also shared many unfortunate events, pains, and laughter. His leaving makes me sad. I miss him already.

*****

Change is inevitable, I know. Eda and Shant have had their first baby, a boy, whom they named Ivan. He is adorable, and he has brightened our lives. Shant is so proud of him, and Eda takes care of him with such love and tenderness. Josh is getting taller, and I am getting curvier, but Mom is still Mom, and Papa is still working hard.

Tonight, during dinner, we all hear a loud shooting sound. Mom, Josh, and I all jump up from the table and run out to the street. To our surprise, almost every neighbor is also out. I hear murmurs of "What was that?"

"It sounds like shooting."

"What shooting?"

One of the neighbors, a young man, says, "Uh, shooting just like the other neighborhoods."

Another says, "I know. I heard that, too."

I ask them, "What's going on? The news hasn't said anything."

An older man replies, "Of course not. The news is kept hush-hush. People are rising in every city. There have even been killings."

"Killing who?" I ask.

The old man answers, "People who are rising against the Shah. Enough is enough of this dictatorship. The poor get poorer and the rich get richer. This won't work anymore."

Another neighbor announces, "Enough! Go home before something bad happens!"

In a hushed voice, a woman says, "The walls have rats and the rats have ears." I know she's referring to a neighbor who people think works with SAVAK.

Mom orders us to go back to the house. I hurry inside, turn on Papa's radio, and start playing with the frequency.

"Ariana, what are you doing?" Josh asks.

"I'm trying to find a radio station. Maybe we can get some news."

After messing with the stations and adjusting the radio's antenna, I can finally listen to the BBC. I hear the voice of a British journalist speaking Farsi, but the voice isn't very clear. He says,

"There are reports of the killing of innocent civilians by the Shah's military. People in different cities of Iran are protesting and are ready to strike. The Iranians are rising."

And that's when I lose the radio frequency. With only thoughts of the strike and killing, I fall asleep.

The next day in school, the conversations of my teachers, mostly Miss Danash, my literature teacher, are about the revolution. "You all," she says, "should be supportive of the many people in different cities and go to strike, too."

One of my classmates, Noosh, says, "Ma'am, but we are Armenian, and we're the minority."

"That is true, but you live in this country, and you are part of it. Freedom is for all," she claims with passion.

"But how can we have freedom?" I ask Miss Danash.

She answers firmly, "With unity."

Another student adds, "But we are free. Look at us! We go to school, we learn our Bible, and we have music, disco, and TV!"

Miss Danash looks at my classmate with chagrin, saying, "These things aren't real freedom. Look at the life of the farmer, who works so hard from the crack of dawn to dusk. Then the landlord takes all his earnings, leaving him in a shack with very little to take care of his family, perhaps without running water or doctors. Freedom is expressing your thoughts and beliefs. Freedom is reading a book about differing political viewpoints. Freedom is being able to choose your leader."

The class bell rings, but no one moves. My teacher's words sink in. This is just the beginning, of that I am certain.

1977–1979
The Rising

THE NEWS ESCALATES as the strikes spread. One of the most prominent strikes occurs with the shutting down of the bazaar merchants and their Persian rug stores and gold exchanges.

Papa, home from his trip, already knows about the strikes. "The southern cities are completely shut down. With the bazaar in Tehran closed, the country will paralyze."

"So, Papa, what will happen?" I ask.

"I think this is it. Most likely, the strikes will go on, and there will be an official revolution. That means the regime will change."

"Really, Papa? What kind of regime will we have?"

"I don't know. Usually, this kind of movement starts with a leader. So far, no one has been named. We'll have to wait and see."

With the universities shutting down and people becoming more vocal, unity brings more power to the civilians. I feel a newfound strength inside of me. I want to know more, so I begin listening to older students and sitting in on their group meetings. They give me books to read. I feel alert and more aware. I am one of them.

It isn't long before the grade schools begin to strike. Now, students refuse to go to classes. We stay in the courtyard carrying on debates in every corner of the schoolyard. Even with the principal's urging us to get to our classes, we ignore her.

"Politics are not for you. You are here to study. Now get to class or you will fail!" she announces from her booming megaphone.

None of us heeds her warning. We stand our ground, and she retreats to her office.

A big announcement appears through flyers. All are requested to join a march in front of Tehran University tomorrow. I've already read it ten times and I can't wait to show it to Papa!

"Papa, look!" I say, presenting the flyer to him.

"What is it, Ariana?"

"It's an announcement of a big march for freedom. It'll take place in front of Tehran University tomorrow! It says, 'Everyone who believes in freedom should be there.' I'm going!"

"Wait, wait a minute," Papa says, gaining my eyes. "Ariana, you know I am all for freedom, but this is not going to be easy. The Shah has a lot of power with his Special Forces and SAVAK. People will be in danger."

"Papa, I realize that, but if no one goes, and if there is no unity, how will we ever have freedom?"

"Ariana, *Baless*, I am very proud of you. You have become so alert, and you are such a smart girl. I agree with you, but I don't want my clever girl to get hurt. Read books from different ideologies, so you can choose the one you like. If you don't know the differences, how will you know which one you believe in?"

My brain is full of information, and my young soul is eager to make changes. I feel like a seed crying for rain.

*****

Instead of going to school today, I meet up with a big group of friends near our school. Our group leader, Abram, is giving us some tips before we march.

"Listen carefully, guys," he says. "If you have your school books, leave them in the school. Don't carry any ID, and write your blood type on your wrists," and he hands out a permanent marker for us to use. "This is serious. The Shah's Special Forces might be present today and there may be shootings. Stick together and don't lose your group. Follow the bigger groups and repeat only what is asked of you. Remember, this is a calm demonstration."

As Abram finishes his announcement, we follow in silence. People in the street offer their support and prayers of "God be with you!" and "Fight for freedom!"

As we near the university, the crowd grows. I can't believe there are so many people! There must be thousands of demonstrators! The entire boulevard is packed with men and women, young and old. Some carry banners with writing, such as "Freedom, Equality, Unity." Just as the crowd gets bigger, so do the Special Forces. The militia stands with their guns ready.

Suddenly, by the order of their commander, they air shoot. The demonstrators only get louder, singing, "Freedom! Freedom!" and "Down with the Shah!"

I repeat what I hear, but inside, I'm so scared. I've never heard shooting so close to me before, nor have I been in such a crowd. The din grows louder and angrier. The firing becomes more rapid. Demonstrators are getting separated as the military forcefully pushes through. My friends and I run to the safety of our neighborhood.

At the end of the day, in a news report, I hear some unruly students have been captured by the Shah's police. The news report names them "terrorists." Day after day, the protests cover every city and neighborhood in Iran. Unfortunately, sometimes, it ends in a riot, where the merchants' stores get broken into and looted. No one knows this is an act of the Shah, meant to give the demonstration a bad name.

The Shah's power is evidenced by his military tanks guarding the city's most important buildings. But as the striking continues, they show dissent with carnations in the barrels of their guns and tanks, given to them by civilians.

***

Due to the strikes, there aren't many jobs, so Papa has been home for a while. He succumbs to desperation. "I don't want to break any strikes, but I need to make money to support the family, Ariana."

"What are you going to do, Papa? How long will it take before the Shah is defeated?"

"I don't know, *Baless*."

"Papa, you know I like you being home."

My Dream

IT ISN'T LONG BEFORE Papa finds out there is merchandise available for transportation in the city of Karmanshah, a mountainous province northwest of Tehran. Papa seems happy. He calls Uncle Andy (Auntie Lydia's husband and Irene and Annie's father), with whom he travels, to give him the news.

The next day, Papa and Andy leave for Karmanshah. Early in the morning, I hear Papa say, "Liz, be careful and don't let the kids in the streets. It's dangerous."

"We'll be all right. You take care of yourself."

Still in bed, I listen closely to Papa and Mom's conversation. I hear worry.

***

Chaos surrounds us, and I've even heard of casualties.

After two weeks of worrying about Papa and his safety, Uncle Miktar, Papa's brother, arrives at our house with news. "The guys at my garage told me Andy and Jacob were seen a few days ago, but there is no work for them as they were promised."

"Are they coming back?" Mom asks.

"I think they've decided to leave their trailer trucks there and come home by train," Uncle Miktar replies.

"Why don't they drive back?" I ask.

Uncle Miktar replies, "I guess there's no fuel for the trucks because of the strikes."

With the news of Papa's safety, I get ready for bed.

I hear my uncle say, "Liz, let's go over to Ted's house. I haven't seen him in a while."

"That sounds good. I will go with you."

I hear the door close, and I think to myself how odd it is for them to go to Uncle Ted's so late at night . . . and so suddenly.

***

The annoying sound of my alarm clock wakes me at 6:45. I sit up in my bed, undo my long, twisted nightgown, then turn and place my feet on the floor. As I put my hands to my forehead, the unwelcome guest of last night's strange dream revisits my memory.

With an uneasy feeling, I get up and change into my denim pants and a navy-blue shirt. I drag myself to the bathroom to wash up and brush my short hair, then head to the kitchen for breakfast.

"Grandma? Hi! How is it you're here so early in the morning?"

"Well, can't I come to see my granddaughter?"

"Of course, you can, Grandma. Wait a minute. You actually spent the night in our house?" I know something is up now.

"Yes, I did. Why are you so surprised?"

"Well, because last time you spent the night was when Mom had her eye surgery and I was just seven years old. That was ten years ago."

Mom broke our conversation by asking if I wanted eggs for breakfast.

"No, thank you, Mom." *Why is she being nice to me? What is she up to?*

Without planning to, as I drink my tea, I say, "Grandma, I had a strange dream last night."

Since she's very good at translating dreams, she folds her arms and gives me all her attention. "What did you see? I'm sure I'll have a good answer for you."

"I dreamt of a long, narrow corridor. Fire was everywhere. There was chaos around me. As I ran toward a door, which had square windows in it, I reached for a silver-colored door handle and tried to open it. Suddenly, Papa grabs me from behind, trying to pull me away. I screamed, 'Papa, someone I know is inside! I have to rescue him!' Papa pulled me away, saying, 'No, let go! No, you can't!'

"Grandma, do you know what my dream means?"

"Girl, maybe you had too much to eat last night!" She chuckles anxiously.

Mom looks puzzled. "That's enough, Ariana. You'll be late for school."

"You're right. I'm leaving."

Even though my school is on strike, I still have to attend my midterm tests. The entire walk to school leaves me thinking something just isn't right. I can feel it in my bones. All day long, I have a strange feeling.

I get to school and head to my classroom, where I see my cousins. Together, we walk to the third floor.

"I wish I could go home," I say to Irene and Anna. Then I tell them about my dream.

"You have such crazy dreams!" Irene shakes her head.

Finally, the three o'clock bell rings. I rush home, feeling nauseous.

"Hi, Mom," I say, walking into the kitchen.

"Hi, Ariana. How was school?" Mom asks in an almost-sweet voice.

"Same as always. No teachers, no class, but I still had exams."

"Ariana, I need to tell you something." As we sit at the kitchen table, I wait on pins and needles to hear what she is about to say. "Ariana, we have to be thankful to the Lord your father is safe."

I interrupt her. "Mom, has there been a bomb explosion on a train?" I scare myself remembering the details in my dream. "Oh my

God, Mom?" I continue with such a rush. "Oh Mom, no! My dream! I saw Papa in a train. Then there was an explosion and fire. Please don't lie to me. Is my papa safe? Is he alive!?"

Mom places her hand on my shoulder. "Yes, Ariana. Your father is safe. He called last night. That's why Uncle Miktar asked me to go to Uncle Ted's house."

"I knew something was wrong. I just knew it!"

"Ariana, how could you have had such a vivid dream?"

"I don't know. What about Uncle Andy?" She didn't have to tell me. I already knew.

"Ariana, perhaps the person you were trying to save in your dream was Uncle Andy."

I sit back in the chair limply, weeping openly. *How could this happen?* I jump up quickly. "Mom, does Auntie Lydia know? What about Irene and Annie?" I hurry toward the door.

"Wait, Ariana. Where are you going?"

"To see my cousins. They need me."

Mom grabs Josh, and the three of us leave together for Auntie Lydia's house.

"Mom, do they know?"

"Yes, Ariana. I was there all day."

As I worry for Irene and Annie, I question myself. *How is it that Mom cares so much for others in a time of tragedy?* But this question is overshadowed by wondering how I will comfort my cousins, knowing my papa is safe and theirs is not.

Inside Auntie Lydia's house, a big crowd is gathered. While everyone tries their best to comfort one another, I go to Irene and Annie's bedroom. They are both sitting on the edges of their beds in silence.

"Oh, Irene. I'm so sorry," I say, trying not to cry. I hold Annie tightly, and we sit there in a long embrace. They are so quiet. I think they must be in shock, trying to deny the terrible tragedy.

Annie says, "Ariana, when you told me your dream this morning, I thought you were crazy. I even laughed at you."

"No worries, Annie. I wish it would stay a crazy dream."

Together, we cry.

Irene asks, "So what really happened? How bad were my father's injuries?"

"I don't know, Irene. I think the only one who knows is my papa."

We share our grief until late into the night.

***

Upon arriving home, I ask Mom, "When is Papa coming home?" I can't convince myself that Papa is safe until I see him.

Mom explains that Uncle Miktar and some of Papa's friends are going to catch a flight to Karmanshah, where they will bring home Papa and Uncle Andy's remains.

I go to my bed, lie down, and close my eyes, trying to process it all, hoping that when I wake up, it will all have been just a dream.

Papa's Story

ON A DARK NIGHT, two long, sad days later, Papa, Uncle Miktar, and Uncle Ted walk into the house. I look at Papa and I can't believe my eyes. His salt and pepper hair seems to have turned whiter. His face has aged and his physical appearance is that of a skinny, hunched-over old man.

I run to him, clinging, sobbing. He caresses my hair, then tilts my head up to look into my eyes. "*Baless*, I am here. I am safe."

"Oh, Papa. I saw you in my dream. You were trapped in a blazing fire!" As I crush my face into his chest, we shake and weep in fear and relief.

Mom separates us. "All right, Ariana. Let him take a shower and change. He needs to rest."

After Papa has showered and changed, and Mom has tried encouraging him to eat, Eda and Shant join us. Little Ivan had stayed home with Shant's parents.

Papa shares a glass of whiskey with the other uncles and Shant, then begins to tell the story. His laugh is painful, the kind people do when they have too much hurt in their heart, and his eyes get a sad, faraway look, as if he is watching a nightmare transpire all over again. "Well, as the strike was going on, there was no fuel for all our trucks. We stayed, thinking maybe the next day we'd get some. But instead, the strike lasted longer, and we began to run out of money. That's when Andy insisted we leave and come home by train. At first, I disagreed, but Andy persisted, and I gave in.

"We bought our train tickets, boarded the train, found our cabin, and started settling in. A young man walked into our cabin with a duffel bag and left it in a corner. As he was leaving, in quite the rush, I jokingly yelled at him, saying, 'Hey, buddy, where are you going? You left your bag. There isn't a bomb in it, is there?' The strange guy disappeared, leaving us thinking he would come back and maybe share the cabin with us.

"Anyway, I took my shoes off, and as Andy got up to get a drink, I asked him, 'Hey Andy, get me something, too!'

"He left and came back without a drink for me, so, I said, 'Man, you didn't bring me anything?'

"'Oh, I forgot,' Andy said.

"That's when I got up to get myself one, and he said, 'Hey, Jacob. Give me your reading glasses and the extra money you have. I can't trust you. You'll get robbed!'"

Papa stops talking for a minute, sips his whiskey, and wipes away the tears starting to fall. "Andy sat on *my bench*, took *my reading glasses*, the newspaper, and what little money we had on us, and I left to go get my drink."

It's so quiet it seems like no one is even breathing.

Papa clears his throat and swallows hard. "I had walked to the next car when I heard it. A deafening explosion. I turned back, but all I could see was a blazing fire. I ran toward it. I reached for the door handle. All I could feel was the intense heat and all I could see through the window were flames. I screamed for Andy, but the guard pulled me away and took me outside. People were running around screaming as smoke and dust permeated the air. I sat on the ground and noticed the bottom of the cabin had collapsed." Papa sips his whiskey again. His eyes frozen and his hands trembling, he looks as if he'd seen a ghost. Inhaling harshly through his nose, trying not to cry, he says, "And I saw something on the ground melting away. It was . . . it was . . ."

"Oh, enough, Jacob! My God, what you've witnessed!" Mom exclaims, putting a halt to his description.

Everything I've heard makes my stomach turn, but I want to know everything my dear papa has been through. I want to feel what he felt.

Papa closes his eyes, remembering, tears flowing freely down his cheeks. "I found myself wandering around without shoes or money on me. A policeman approached me, took my hand, and gave me some water to drink. I said to him, 'I saw the guy's face.'

"The policeman told me, 'Forget it. He's long gone. Stay here with me. As soon as the bodies are transferred to the hospital, I will take you there so you can identify your friend.'

"I corrected him by saying, 'He is my cousin.'

"As the policeman took me to the hospital, I desperately tried to collect myself. I walked down a long hallway with tens of dead bodies covered in white sheets lying side by side on the floor. Around me were the lamenting cries of people calling their loved ones by name. As I dragged my heavy, tired feet on the cold hospital floor, from a distance, I saw a man with a body built like Andy and black glasses like mine. I screamed, 'Andy! Andy, it's me! Come here!' And I waved at him.

"The man came closer, placed his hand on my shoulder, and said, 'Monsieur, I am not Andy.' His face was full of such compassion.

"Then a nurse came over to me. 'Monsieur, let me help you find your relative.' And with the nurse's guidance, after checking many dead bodies, I found the remains of Andy. All that was recognizable were my broken glasses and a pocket watch with a piece of money stuck to it. I leaned in closer to check what I already knew I would find . . . the initials A.M."

Papa reaches into his overcoat pocket, takes out the pocket watch, which is wrapped in a clear piece of plastic, and stares at it blankly. Uncle Miktar takes the bag out of Papa's hand and passes it to everyone in the room. Papa lights a cigarette, inhales deeply, and slowly lets it out, watching it as it swirls in the air, then takes a sip of whiskey.

He is quiet.

For days.

***

The pain of losing Uncle Andy is unfathomable. Our family is wracked with denial. How can anyone believe he died in an act of terrorism? He was a happy soul, excited to come home to his family. Then he vanishes in a bomb blast.

On the day of the funeral, all my friends from school and our assistant principal, Mr. Varouj, whom we call Mr. V, are present at the cemetery. We're all dressed in our school uniforms: a light-blue, button-down shirt, navy-blue skirt, and white stockings. The boys have on their long navy pants with their own blue, button-down shirts. We assemble in two groups, side by side. Karo, one of my classmates, and I are first in line, holding a big wreath of white carnations with a wide black ribbon across it. We are followed by Mr. V and my other classmates. Annie and Irene are already there with their mom, Auntie Lydia.

We walk toward the burial site where the priest stands holding his Bible and cross, and the deacon beside him burns frankincense in a brass-hanging censer, praying over the coffin. My poor papa is the only one who knows the secret in the box. My heart drops, seeing Auntie Lydia all dressed in black, and Irene and Annie standing stoically beside her.

As unbearable as my profound sadness is for my cousins, I thank God for keeping my papa safe for me.

An Unlikely Gang

THESE LAST FEW MONTHS have been rough, especially with Uncle Andy's death. Each day I see Papa sad, quiet, and guilt-ridden. Guilty for not being able to save Uncle Andy, and seeing Auntie Lydia in sorrow, who now must raise her daughters all by herself with no money coming home. All she can do is sew for people.

Armenian tradition honors those who have passed by refraining from decorating for Christmas. Because of our family's loss, this includes us. Christmas is not a celebrated holiday in Iran, so Armenian schools usually only have one day off. But because of this year's political circumstances, we are getting three days off!

Our principal, Miss Nadia, arrives to visit our classroom a few days later. As she enters the room with our favorite assistant principal, Mr. V, we all stand to show respect.

She says, "Take a seat. Good morning. Everyone knows this year we have a long holiday."

"Yay!" we all cheer.

With a serious look, Miss Nadia smacks her hand on the desk. "Keep quiet! I am here to tell you students, do not attempt to hang any decorations in the classroom! If I find any, the entire class will be suspended for two weeks." After making her bold statement, she and Mr. V leave.

We mumble under our breaths as our economics teacher, Mr. Said, draws our attention to his notes written on the blackboard. He whistles sharply as we busily copy the notes. I turn my head to the right and stare at my three guy friends, who sit next to each other—Karo, whose nickname is "Blue"; David, whom I call "Moustache"; and Danny, a.k.a. "Curly."

This trio consists of the naughtiest boys in the entire school. And yes, they have an accomplice, who happens to be the most trusted, loveable girl amongst the students, just because she never gets caught. This girl, of course, is me.

As soon as recess breaks, Blue, Moustache, Curly, and I meet up at the school cafeteria.

"What was that nonsense Miss Nadia was talking about?" Karo says.

Moustache adds, "But it's Christmas! We have to celebrate! Plus, we need to brighten the mood in our class, especially for Annie."

"What if we do decorate our classroom?" I bravely ask.

Curly replies, "What if Miss Nadia comes and checks our room?"

Blue answers, "Ahh, I don't think she'll come to our class on the third floor twice in one month."

"You're right, Blue," I say. "Let's plan. We only have tomorrow. We have a bunch of Christmas lights at home we never use."

Curly adds, "I'll bring ribbons and flocking."

"I'll bring ornaments!" says Blue.

Moustache, who has been quiet till now, declares, "And I'll have a surprise!"

We all look at him with cocked eyebrows.

"What surprise?" I ask.

"Well, if I say, it won't be a surprise then, will it?"

"Whatever." Curly shrugs and shoves his hands in his pockets.

Blue suggests, "Well, we won't tell anyone until tomorrow. First thing in the morning, we'll start decorating."

"Great!" I say. "But I think we should come early."

"It's a plan!" we all agree.

***

When I get home, Mom is out, so I go to our storage room and quickly put together the old Christmas lights, some markers, and pieces of cardboard. I pack them all in a black garbage bag and hide it under my bed.

Josh quietly watches me and asks, "Ariana, what are you doing?"

"Shh, Josh. I'm taking these Christmas lights to school tomorrow to decorate our classroom. You have to keep it a secret. You must not tell Mom. You know if she finds out, she'll be very upset."

"I know, Ariana. I promise I won't tell."

All night long, I think about the Christmas lights under my bed. *Oh, it'll be so much fun to have a decorated classroom!*

***

In the morning, while Mom is in the kitchen, I sneak out the garbage bag filled with Christmas lights and crafts. "Mom, I have to go in early today. I'm going to study for a test with my friends."

"Eat something first."

"No, Mom, I have to go." And I run outside carrying the heavy trash bag, holding it with both hands to my chest.

I finally get to school and trudge up the three flights of stairs to my classroom. Behind me comes Moustache, dragging a big, old Christmas tree. My heart stops. "Oh my God! Are you crazy?"

He snickers. "It's not Christmas without a Christmas tree!"

Blue and Curly walk in with pep in their step and go straight over to high-five Moustache.

"You, my friend, are a genius!" Blue says to Moustache.

Curly asks, "How'd you get through Karry?"

Karry is the old man who stands near the main school entrance. He's always there to open or close the door for us. The school provides him with a small room in which he lives. No one knows his name, so he is everyone's "Karry."

Moustache explains, "It wasn't hard. I gave him a pack of my dad's cigarettes."

We all giggle.

"Moustache, you've got some guts!" I affirm, watching him run out of the classroom as if he's forgotten something.

While we are busy attaching the ribbons to the walls, Moustache comes back with a big tin bucket filled with dirt. Blue, Curly, and I stop and stare.

"What is that?" Curly asks.

I figure it out quickly. "Well, of course we can't leave the tree leaning against the wall."

Blue helps Moustache plant the tree in the tin bucket full of dirt.

"Now we have a Christmas tree!" Moustache says.

We jump in and start decorating our tree. Moustache and Curly get busy wrapping Christmas lights around it, while Blue and I add fifty colorful ornaments. We counted them all!

Other students begin walking into the classroom. Many of them call us crazy.

Then, one by one, they start asking if they can help.

"Of course!" I sing out joyfully. "You guys can spray the windows with flocking. Also, I have cardboard and markers. Get creative! We don't have much time, and we must make sure the classroom door stays closed."

Blue adds, "Yeah, and no *fish* allowed!"

By the time the first period bell rings, every inch of the classroom is covered with colorful ribbons and bows. Cut-out paper snowflakes adorn each window, but the greatest decoration of all is the lit Christmas tree.

Once everyone arrives, the whole class smiles with pride and joy. Even our teacher, Mr. Said, and Annie grin.

By the end of the day, we make sure the lights are unplugged and shut the door behind us before we head home for our three-day holiday.

"Merry Christmas!" I wish to everyone.

***

Upon returning from Christmas break, we are still enjoying the decorations, so we decide to keep them up for the rest of the week. Each day, we watch our green tree turn more and more yellow. Meanwhile, most students in the school know about our secret. Some sneak into our classroom to check out our masterpiece. The other juniors and seniors keep our secret, but ultimately, word gets out.

At the end of the week, Miss Nadia decides to check our classroom one more time. Without notice, she walks in and places her hand on her chest as if having a heart attack. She frantically says one word, "Suspended!" And with short, quick steps, she leaves. We are left speechless.

Our assistant principal, Mr. V, comes in shortly thereafter, looks around, and states, "I don't need to ask who the mastermind was behind this. I already know. Now start cleaning up. I don't want to see the tiniest trace of decoration. Saturday, we will talk about your suspensions." And he abruptly leaves.

"Oh, no!" echoes around me. Some girls protest, saying, "We never agreed to this. Whoever did this should clean up."

Blue says, "Sorry, it doesn't work that way."

I nod in agreement and firmly add, "You all enjoyed it just as much, so you are just as guilty!"

No teachers come to class today as we take down every decoration and scrub the flocking-covered windows. Of course, it wasn't nearly as fun tearing it all down as it was putting it up.

As our job seems near its end, Blue, Moustache, Curly, and I stare at the dried-up yellow Christmas tree.

"What are we going to do with this?" Curly asks.

Moustache says, "We'll take it out on Saturday. Let's go home."

I take back the old Christmas lights in the same way I had brought them, hoping Mom never finds out about my sneaking around behind her back. But mostly, I keep thinking about how in the world we are going to get rid of the tree in the classroom.

***

Saturday, as soon as the first bell rings, Mr. V arrives to our class. "I hope you are ready for your suspension. First, get rid of this tree, then everyone will stay in the classroom for the entire school day without a teacher, and you will copy every one of your study books. The only time you may leave is for your thirty-minute lunch break. I will frequently check in on you. When I come back, I don't want to find a single needle fallen from this tree." He gives each of us a stern glare, then leaves.

Because Mr. V is respected and loved, no one protests. When it's finally time for our lunch break, most of us gather in the cafeteria since it's so cold outside, although a few insist on playing out in the snow. Right then, one of the freshmen runs into the cafeteria screaming, "Fire! Fire!"

We hurry outside. A freshman points to the third floor.

Oh my God! That's my classroom!

Black smoke escapes around the edges of the window. Mr. V runs to the stairwell with a fire extinguisher in hand, with several teachers on his heels. I frantically search for Blue, Curly, and Moustache, but they are nowhere to be seen.

I sprint into the school where I see them hurrying toward me. "What happened?"

Curly responds with uncontrollable laughter.

More firmly, I ask again, "Moustache, *what happened*?" Before he can respond, I continue, "Did you set fire to the tree?"

Blue answers between giggles, "Well, that was the easiest way to get rid of it," eyeing the lighter in his hand.

"Oh my God! You guys are out of your minds! You could have set fire to the whole school! You idiots!"

Eventually, Mr. V and the teachers put out the flames. Now, the entire building smells like smoke and our classroom is coated in a black haze. The smoke has permeated the walls, the benches, and our belongings. Needless to say, we are all disappointed at how our happy place has gone up in smoke.

The rest of the day, and for the next two weeks, we sit outside in the courtyard with a volunteer teacher to study. The only time we can move into the cafeteria is when it snows. Besides that, every hour, one group heads up to our classroom to clean and paint the walls and benches. It's quite the punishment. But even under these circumstances, our young spirits are lifted, all because of an unlikely gang.

1979–1983
Calm

THE TELEVISION STATIONS are now controlled by the people, instead of the Shah's government. Journalists jump at the opportunity to film from the inside of the SAVAK prison when activists boldly break in. They witness firsthand the torture chambers and the tools used against its prisoners. Inside one of the chambers, a news reporter finds handcuffs mounted to the ceiling, blood stains on the floor, and the equipment to inflict electrical shock. The men and women who endured so much are now freed. SAVAK is no more.

The living room is silent. None of us talks. I am in disbelief at what these activists went through for freedom, but at the same time, I'm relieved it is over. Papa shakes his head, cursing the Shah under his breath. Occasionally, Mom murmurs, and Josh, who sits on the floor close to the TV screen, looks puzzled.

"What is the Shah going to do now, Papa?" I ask.

"He's going to leave. But where to? I don't know. He's like a stray dog now. He burned bridges with America, so they surely won't take him in."

"How about Europe?" asks Mom.

Papa answers, "I'm not sure about Europe, but most likely Egypt. It will be interesting to see where he ends up."

It isn't long before news breaks of the royal family fleeing Iran. The reporter approaches the Shah and Shah Bano (the queen) as they are getting ready to step into their private jet. The reporter asks, "Do you have anything to say to what was once your country?"

With tearful eyes, the Shah answers, "I am leaving and taking three things with me: safety, wealth, and joy." Then they board their jet.

The reporter enthusiastically announces, "Congratulations, Iran!"

The entire country—every city, every neighborhood—is in celebration. Civilians give carnations to the Shah's military and decorate their tanks with tossed flowers. Everyone chants, "Run away, Shah! Run away!"

With his leaving, every political group feels the victory, the freedom for all. Now it's time for the new leader. Rumor has it, his name is Khomeini.

"Who is Khomeini?" I ask Papa.

All he says is, "He is an Islamic leader who was exiled to France fourteen or fifteen years ago by the Shah."

"Papa, is he a good leader?"

"That's a big question. He has been preaching Islam all his life."

"You think he's an extremist?"

"From what I know, he will be. I hope I'm wrong, *Baless*."

Every day, I hear Khomeini's name more and more. The streets of Iran are still in turmoil. Some of the Shah's military continue to try to defend parts of the city, especially the palaces. But despite the majority of the military disobeying the exited dictator, there are still shootings, tear gas episodes, burning tires, and demonstrations.

The city is a battlefield, and the curfew remains in effect. Every organization, whether it be Communist, liberal, or Islamic, has their mottos written on the walls. Military tanks position themselves around the university, along with barricades and soldiers ready to fire. Everyone is waiting, waiting for Khomeini's arrival.

***

The telephone rings. I pick up the phone. "Hello?"

"Hello, Ariana. I just took Eda to the hospital. She's in labor."

I hold the receiver away from my face and yell, "Mom! Mom! Eda's in the hospital!"

In a rush, Mom grabs the phone and says, "Okay, just honk when you're here. I'll come outside."

When Shant arrives, they go to be with Eda as she gives birth to their second child.

Meanwhile, I stay home with Josh, who has a million questions I cannot answer about Eda. We are coloring.

"Ariana, where is Eda?" Josh stops to look at my reaction.

"At the hospital."

"Why?"

"Well, she is about to have her baby."

"How is she going to have her baby?"

Oh, boy . . . "Josh, at the hospital, the doctor will cut her belly a little bit so the baby can be born."

Josh pauses, thinking hard. "So what happens if she doesn't go to the hospital? Would her belly burst open?"

Hmmmm . . . How do I answer him? "No, Josh, her belly won't burst. It's just if the doctor opens her belly, it will be less painful. That's why Shant took her to the hospital."

That stopped the inquisition. I don't know if I convinced him or if he just gave up.

***

At the end of the day, Mom comes home with the news of Eda and her baby.

"What is it, Mom? A boy or a girl?" I've been waiting all day for this!

Mom replies, "A beautiful baby girl with big blue eyes, just like her dad."

"What did they name her?"

"They chose Maral."

"I like it! How is Eda?" I am quite concerned for my big sister.

"She's fine," Mom says with very little emotion. "The doctor will release her tomorrow."

"Mom, how were the streets around the hospital? I was so worried."

"It's calm, but the military is still everywhere. And there are a lot of burnt tires to diffuse the tear gas." She busies herself. "The sooner Eda goes home, the safer she will be."

***

Eda's baby girl, Maral, is a week old, and today broadcasting announces the new leader, Khomeini, will arrive in Iran tomorrow. The country chants and cheers, the streets are getting cleaned up, and the military has backed off. They have even announced their support for Khomeini. Excitement is in the air!

The curfew is over, and the merchants decorate the outsides of their stores with myriads of colorful hanging lights and flowering baskets. The country's roads resemble vibrant firecrackers ready to be launched, as we await our new leader.

Once again, every city, every neighborhood, is in celebration. Busy streets and cheerful people congratulate one another. The bakers hand out fresh-baked goods and grocers offer candies and flowers. I am ecstatic to witness the transformation in my city from one politically repressed to one politically free.

Papa, Mom, Josh, and I watch the news reporting Khomeini's arrival from Mehrabad International Airport, which has not hosted so many people at once in its entire existence. Crowds hold banners and carry flags plastered with Khomeini's picture on them.

When the Air France vessel carrying Khomeini lands, he steps out to wave at followers surrounding the plane and his guards. Their din of support is clear in their cries, *"Allah Akbar!"* (God is great!)

By the force of his guards, the new leader enters a waiting car, but the crowd is so dense, it is unable to move. The news reporter explains how the guards were forced to lift the car off the ground and carry it as if it were a throne.

As Khomeini arrives, he speaks to the entire country, promising the freedoms of religion, of different parties, and shutting down the Shah's prisons. The speech brings a joy and trust to the people. A city once torn by a storm slowly begins to show signs of calm. The sun pushes the dark clouds away.

The mood in the streets is light as I walk to school, where normal classes have resumed. On my way, I see young adults setting up their books and fliers at the street corners, inviting pedestrians to join their political groups. The physical change of my country delights me. I only wish Matthew and Uncle Andy were here to witness it, too.

Gregory

WITH THE SHAH GONE and Khomeini's arrival, the country has a different atmosphere. There is more freedom than anyone could ever ask for and the streets are cleaned up. The latest talk is of general voting, in which all are free to vote, to choose an Islamic Republic or not. The voters only have to circle their vote, yes or no.

The entire neighborhood rushes to their voting sites. I'm so excited! It is my first time to vote. Actually, it's everyone's first time. Standing in a long line, chitchatting with people, I sense hushed voices. By the looks on their faces, they seem unhappy and disappointed. I overhear complaints of why the only question on the ballot is whether or not to choose an Islamic Republic.

What about other leaders? I keep quiet as the whispers continue.

In just a few days, the announcement is made. By a majority of votes, the government has been chosen. It is an Islamic Republic, and the leader is Khomeini.

Life has gone back to normal, except with much political freedom. Also, with Khomeini as leader, he announces everyone who has died during the Revolution will be recognized as a martyr, and to their memories, there will be a memorial vigil in the neighborhood. Of course, these vigils are only for *male* martyrs. Their pictures are recognized in *hejleh*, an Islamic tradition where a tall display stands decorated with tens of small lights and flowers, honoring the deceased. Uncle Andy is one of them, even though he was Armenian. This means the new government will financially help Auntie Lydia.

It seems like everything is going in the right direction. People are happy, and Papa has more jobs. And, as always, I wait for him to come home every day so we can watch the news, and I can learn more from him. Most importantly, Mom can't go on a rampage when he is home.

Meanwhile, the new government is established and changes are taking place. Changes that at first seemed promising, but have soon become contradictory. The new Islamic Republic law does not recognize any political organization unless it is Islamic, and the Left parties are considered Atheist, which is forbidden in Islam. Therefore, no such groups are allowed to exist, and if there is any activity, the members will be prosecuted.

Learning the new law, I sometimes worry for a family friend I have known since my childhood. I know their only child, a son named Gregory, has strong beliefs as a Chappy, a Communist. Apparently, he has a mind of his own. He works hard and spends every dime helping poor families. Despite his parents' plea for him to end his involvement, not only because it breaks the new law but because it's also very dangerous, Gregory refuses to quit his work . . . That is, until one day, when rumors start that Gregory has been captured by Islamic brothers.

Mom and I decide to go and visit the family. As we do, Mrs. Mari welcomes us into her house. Worry for her only child is etched on her face.

"Is it true?" Mom asks.

Mrs. Mari is trembling in sorrow. "Yes, it is true. So many times, Albert and I begged him to stop what he was doing. We didn't want him to get into trouble, but he didn't listen to us." She covers her mouth with her hand, shaking her head, overwrought with grief.

I ask Mrs. Mari, "Do you know when he'll be released?"

She manages to calm herself slightly. "Soon. Actually, I think he'll call us when his prosecution is over."

"Oh, that is good," I say.

Mom offers comfort by adding, "I hope you don't have to wait long and that it is all over very soon."

Later, on our way home, Mom says, "Poor woman. She is worried sick."

"I know, Mom. I hope Gregory comes home soon."

***

A week has passed since we visited Mrs. Mari, when I see one of my old classmates, Gisele, who lives in the same apartment complex as Mrs. Mari. We greet each other with a hug. She whispers in my ear, "Have you heard?"

"Heard what?'

She grabs my arm and gets real close to me, as if she wants to make sure no one can hear her.

I ask again, "Heard what, Gisele?"

She steers me closer to the sidewalk wall and answers, "Mrs. Mari's son—"

"What? Is he freed?"

Gisele's countenance is overcome with fear and sadness. "No, no, he isn't freed."

Hesitantly, I search her eyes and grab her arm. I know it's not good news. "Gisele, tell me! What's going on?"

She wails as I pull her close, trying to calm her down enough to give me the news I don't want to hear.

Gisele's words pound in my head. "Gregory has been executed."

"What? Why? I saw Mrs. Mari last week and she was hopeful Gregory would be released soon!"

Gisele whispers, "Because he admitted he was Communist and he wouldn't give up his beliefs. He even claimed he would do it all over again. Therefore, he was recognized as anti-government and sentenced to death."

I am in complete shock. "Oh no! How is Mrs. Mari? Have you seen her?"

"I have. I saw her right after she was given the news on the phone." Gisele sniffled. "I heard an agonizing scream from her apartment. My mom and I ran to her to find her door was open." Gisele pauses a moment to gather her thoughts. "There she was, sitting on the chair, still holding the phone in her hand, wailing, 'My son! My baby! Oh, Gregory! My Gregory, come to me, baby!'"

Gisele conveys an image of Mrs. Mari hitting the phone to her chest and sobbing.

"I left. I couldn't stand to see her like that. My mom spent the rest of the day with her. Ever since, she has locked herself and her husband, Mr. Albert, inside the apartment to mourn. All the neighbors hear them crying and calling Gregory's name as if he could return."

The sorrow I feel for Gregory reaches my soul. I had no idea how staunch Gregory was in his beliefs. I find it so sad he didn't get to say goodbye to his parents and that he would not have a funeral service, only a private memorial. But Gregory made his mark. He died for what he believed in, and for this, his legacy will always be remembered.

Hostages

STILL FEELING THE STING on my cheek Mom's slap left behind, I pick up the broken pieces of the glass I dropped in the kitchen. Her words cut through me, over and over again in my mind, *You clumsy slut!*

My focus shifts from the broken shards of glass to the intense picture on TV. "Mom, Mom, come!" I call.

"What now?"

"Look, it's the American Embassy!"

Papa walks in just as the news breaks. It seems a group of students are trying to get into the American Embassy.

"Who are these people? The students wouldn't do that!" I say with sincere denial.

The screen shows them climbing up the iron gates, jerking and attempting to open them. Then a group manages to get inside! I watch in disbelief as a reporter's camera focuses between the iron gates. Employees of the embassy are blindfolded, handcuffed, and forced into a car.

"Papa, what is going on? Why can't they just let them go back to America?"

He shakes his head in disbelief. "It's too late now. They should have left a long time ago."

"So, what happens next?" I ask, wringing my hands.

"I don't know. There must be some kind of negotiation. This is the end of our friendship with America. Most likely, when the presidency changes, the hostages will be released."

As I watch and listen to Papa, an anchor of sadness overwhelms me. I think of these helpless, hopeless people who will remain isolated from the outside world and away from their families, and my heart aches.

***

The media is constantly updating the hostage situation, but many, including myself, are distracted by more restrictions. As the new government becomes more established, it's announced that textbook changes will be enforced for the upcoming school year. This is followed by the news that the universities might possibly shut down for a few years. I go to Papa to find out what it all means.

"Papa, why are they closing the universities?"

He murmurs with a blank look on his face, "They are cleaning house. Most likely, they want to make sure all the students who are not Islamist are rejected and may even be imprisoned."

"What happened to freedom for all parties?"

With a furrowed brow, Papa says, "There is one party now, and all textbooks will be changed to reflect their agenda, with no eastern or western influence."

I am confused and disappointed. As if these changes and restrictions aren't enough, today, our nation feels the real bombing.

***

In the early afternoon, as I stand halfway up a ladder painting the kitchen walls, Tuscan orange as Mom has demanded, I hear a shrill-sounding noise from outside. I jump down with panic and rush outside to the alley with Mom and Josh. I hear cracking noises in windows as we run outside, where all of our neighbors are gathered. *"Allah Akbar!"* fills the air.

As I hold Josh close to me, the next door neighbor uneasily approaches Mom. "Madam, what is this?"

Mom replies, "I have no idea."

Another young man, who happened to be in the military during the Shah's reign, blurts, "It was a bomb! I know for a fact it sounded like an explosion."

The chant *"Allah Akbar!"* rings around me. "What bomb?" I ask.

Anxious neighbors each have their own idea.

"Maybe it's a terrorist?"

"Maybe it was the refinery?"

No one really knows.

We go back to our houses without answers. I head straight to Papa's radio and play with the frequency as he and I always do. I come across a station playing Arabic dance music. When the song finishes, a spokesperson addresses the Iranian nation. "Iranians, listen carefully. This is Radio Iraq. Our heroic air force has bombed your land."

"Mom!" I yell loudly. "Come listen!"

I motion to the radio right as the announcer says, "We have demolished six different targets from the ports and refineries to the International Mehrabad Airport."

I am speechless, and so is Mom. Soon, the Arabic dance music starts up again. "Mom, it's war!" I declare with shock in my voice.

Josh, who is quietly sitting on the floor, stares at me with brimming eyes. I squeeze him and tousle his wavy hair. "Don't worry, Josh. It'll be over soon." But in my heart, I am extremely troubled. All I know of war is what I've seen in movies, and it's not pretty.

***

Days pass with renewed panic. Broadcasters notify listeners of Iran to learn the different sirens. The high alert siren is constant, whereas the short, staccato one signals safety. We are also encouraged to have a battery-operated radio on at all times, even at night during sleep.

The government tries to keep everything calm and at ease. News releases are becoming few and far between, but people have their ways of getting it from different sources, just like Papa and I do. A few radio stations can be captured by moving the radio's long antennae, which is wrapped with a piece of tin foil, just so. Papa and I listen to BBC, Israel Radio, and now our enemy, Radio Iraq.

Through our next-door Persian neighbor, we learn that even the northern part of the country has been under attack; that many troops have died, as well as many civilian casualties. It is so sad, and there's nothing anyone can do.

In the daytime, the cities seem close to normal, but as the night sky falls, the ear-splitting sounds of enemy fighter jets, either bombing or breaking the sound barrier, fill the air. Thereafter, the sirens wail to alert the city we are under attack.

Mom grabs the prayer book and emergency bag containing our birth certificates, cash, and medication, and I get a flashlight, and along with our neighbors, we run to the basement of our house. This is where we all sit on the ground against the wall, afraid to move. In dim candlelight, the small radio broadcasts news and updates. I hear the anchor say, "Stay calm and sheltered. We are one strong and united country. Nothing and no one can destroy us. God is great!" And patriotic music hums.

One of the neighbors cries while her sister and elderly mother read verses aloud from the Quran. Josh sits next to me, hugging his knees, and Mom is quiet. We continue to hear the bombing from a distance, not knowing the exact location. But the anti-missiles are deafening. After what seems like hours, the radio finally announces we are safe with its staccato alarm.

"Thank God," the elderly woman praises.

With uncertainty, I stand with the others, and we all go back home, just waiting for the next alert.

Since there are many important government buildings surrounding our neighborhood, our house absorbs the incessant booming blasts. During an air strike, the missiles launch one after another; as many as ten, twenty, sometimes even more.

Poor Josh, holding his ears, pale-faced, says bravely to me, "I am not afraid of dying. It's just . . . it's just these noises scare me." I embrace him tightly as tears well up in my eyes. I have to be strong for both of us.

***

Papa comes home tired and dirty. His trip has taken him longer than usual due to the air strikes. As soon as it gets dark, all transportation must stop since they can't turn on their headlights. This would lead the enemy fighter jets to the populated areas. We follow the same routine in the cities—total blackout. By order of the military, every household must cover their windows. This is what I do: I cover every window with layers of newspaper and duct tape in a crisscross shape, in case of an air raid or window rattling. That way if the glass shatters, it won't hurt anyone.

As I finish, I realize how dark and depressing the house looks, especially in the evening as the sun goes down. With a dimly lit candle, we must find our way after sunset, since this is the time the government shuts down the city's power. The darkness is a constant reminder of my own insecurities.

With his dark eyes and dusty gray hair, Papa inspects the house, the windows covered and duct-taped, and mumbles, "What just happened?"

"You mean the war, Papa?"

His head bobs in shock. "Yes. At the port, the refineries have been destroyed. All those beautiful, tall pine trees are now obliterated. There is nothing left in the city; everything is leveled. It's just so sad, *Baless*. War is a nasty thing." With his head down, he walks away to shower.

The bombing becomes a nightly ritual. By morning, civilians go off to work or school and housewives keep up with their chores, but everyone is anxious and scared, including me.

I am a hostage.

No One Wants to Learn

AS MY SENIOR YEAR BEGINS, all the girls from my old school must go to a different school now. Our new one is much larger, especially the cafeteria and gymnasium. But, of course, it is also much farther away, and I have to catch a bus. Otherwise, it would take me an hour and a half to walk, compared to ten minutes to my old school. What I miss the most are my guy friends, my "unlikely gang." There isn't anything we can do about the separation, since Islamic law forbids co-ed classrooms.

As we settle in, we receive our revised textbooks. For the most part, any mentions of the Shah and his kingdom, as well as evolution, have been removed.

We are all flipping through the pages, when one student asks the teacher, "Miss Satou, where is our Bible study book?"

She replies stoically, "Don't worry, we'll get one . . . but it may not be in Armenian."

"What? How can that be?" Meg asks in disbelief.

When our whispers turn to protests, Miss Satou hits the table with her hand. "Keep quiet, everyone! Please, keep quiet. We have to be patient and calm with the changes. Iran has an Islamic government now. We are lucky we have kept our schools, our clubs, and most importantly, our churches. Therefore, we must be compliant about the new restrictions."

Janet, who was quiet until now, says, "Miss Satou, is it true the pictures of the crucified Christ have to be changed and painted showing clothes on Him?"

"What?" I interject. "What nonsense is that? Christ, who endured the beatings and the torture, must now be clothed?"

All at once, everyone has something to say.

Miss Satou raises her hands and in a sharp voice commands, "Quiet!" The chatter ceases. "Yes, I've heard from the officials that will happen."

"So, this is it? It's a done deal?" I ask.

Miss Satou clasps her hands to her chest and replies, "Yes, we must do whatever we can to save our churches."

We soon find out the officials of the church have come to an agreement. White tulle will now cover the painting of the crucifix. All these Islamic rules just don't make sense to me.

*****

Eventually, we get our new religious books. It's some kind of history about Jesus, written in Farsi. No one wants to teach and no one wants to learn. Then we get a book of philosophy, but no teachers have been trained to teach either of these subjects.

We have many new students who have lost their homes in Abadan, the southeast province of Iran, where one of the largest refineries exists. The residents were forced to flee due to bombings. Not fully understanding their devastation, the girls and I welcome them warmly. They tell us stories of how, in a flash, with an uproarious sound, the buildings around them collapsed, and how little time they had to pack up. Instead, they were forced to leave their homes behind, along with all their earthly belongings. Now, they have to start all over again with little or no money. What a sad situation to be in.

Even though our city, the capital, has been bombed, we still have a home. The war hasn't impacted us much. It doesn't seem real. It's one of those things that has to actually happen to you before you can realize the enormity of it.

As we all gather around during lunch, we talk about the F-16 and the Mirage, a French-made fighter jet, and how the Russian *Katyusha* fires so many rockets in a minute. Then we broach the subject of our prepared emergency bags at home, which contain birth certificates, cash, important contact numbers, and medications.

What's going on? We are teenagers in our senior year of high school! We should be full of life, energy, and happiness, making decisions for our future. Instead, we are discussing fighter jet capabilities and emergency preparations. Our once silly conversations about cute boys and mean teachers have shifted to fighter jets? Oh, how our lives have changed.

Hijab

AT TIMES, THE AIR STRIKES stop due to a temporary agreement between Iraq and Iran. During each ceasefire, tensions are less and everyone minds their own business. On one of these days, when I arrive home from school, Eda and her little ones, Ivan and Maral, are at our house.

I hug and kiss Eda, then pick up Ivan in my arms. Little Maral is sound asleep in her bassinet. "Hey, Eda! How is it you come here during the week? You usually visit on the weekend."

Eda pauses to compose herself. "Shant is in prison."

"What? Why?" In my mind, I know Shant is not Chappy or anything else.

"According to Islamic government, it is *haram* for a man to see a woman without *hijab* if she is not a close relative. Since Shant is a hairdresser, his job is forbidden. So last night, while he was at the salon, *komiteh* arrested him."

"Oh my God! What now?"

My sweet Eda, quietly says, "I don't know. I have to wait for his phone call. There's nothing anyone can do."

"I'm so sorry, Eda. I hope he won't get lashed for his sentence."

Mom jumps in, scolding, "God forbid! I hope he is released soon."

For the next thirty days, Eda awaits Shant's phone call, worried sick. By the time Shant is released, Eda looks skinnier than ever.

Thank God, Shant is freed and he was not lashed, but he can no longer be a hairdresser, something he is really good at.

It isn't long before he and Eda decide to leave Iran. France is the fastest way out, so they begin preparing their documents.

***

Once again, the sky ruptures. Bombs fall in place of raindrops. Instead of a clean, fresh essence in the air, there is the scent of gunpowder and death. Last night, all night, our house shook.

Papa picks up Josh as he sleeps, I grab a small flashlight, and Mom retrieves the bag with all our documents inside. Since the officials announced that hiding in basements isn't safe in the case of building collapse, we run downstairs to shelter under the staircase with the rest of the terrified neighbors.

The Persian ladies frantically work to cover their hair with their *hijabs*. One of them asks Papa, "Monsieur, what is going to happen?"

Papa answers, "God is great. We will be fine. Ma'am, most of the noises we hear are anti-aircrafts, but the really loud sounds come from the enemy fighter jets breaking the sound barrier. Our neighborhood is very safe since there are many government buildings surrounding us. The military pays special attention to protect this area."

As the bombing holds everyone in shock, an ear-splitting blast causes us all to cover our ears and bend over with our heads down. The building trembles and the windows reply with a cracking noise. Thank God for the duct tape.

With his back to the door, Papa holds Josh tightly to his chest. I peek at everyone between my fingers. Our Persian neighbors hold each other's hands and mothers cite a prayer from the Quran. The ground shakes beneath me and the wailing siren is relentless. For the next hour, one after another, anti–air missiles defend the city, until another short, pausing siren alerts us the city is now safe. Everyone can return to their homes.

It's two in the morning. Who can go to bed and fall asleep, except for Josh? Although it comforts me to see him back asleep, I am so worried for Eda and her family. No one knows which part of the town has been bombed.

For the rest of the night, I stare at the stars, praying this war will end soon.

***

Oddly enough, early the next morning, we all get on with our lives. Since there has been no damage to our area, all schools, banks, and stores are functioning as normal.

For me, it's almost the end of my senior year. Just a few more finals and I'm done. But with the universities closed, I don't know what I'll do. As if the war and commotion aren't enough, I have to deal with my own battlefield. Mom unleashes her anger daily over every little thing I do. Her satisfaction is complete only when she has humiliated me.

My last two finals are in my "Farsi version" of the Bible and philosophy classes, the latter of which we never had an assigned teacher. Every student is worried. We all head to the testing center, get situated, and within the first ten minutes, everyone walks out turning in a blank sheet.

When it's time to pick up our test scores from school, it doesn't surprise me that most students, including me, have failed both, knowing we never had skilled teachers. Therefore, this summer, we'll have to study and retake them. Lucky for us, though, the superintendent dismisses the philosophy exam results, but I still have to retake the Farsi Bible class. I study so much that I memorize the book word for word. When I retake the exam, I am the only student who scores a perfect score, twenty out of twenty! Yay, me!

***

This afternoon on the news, a new Islamic rule is made known to the citizens. *Hijab* is now mandatory for *all* women. Not only must our hair be covered, but our bodies as well. We are required to wear *roopush*, a long raincoat-type dress, along with long pants, and no makeup or perfume. How can this be?

Shortly after the announcement of *hijab*, thousands of women opposed to this start protesting, which later turns into marching. Against Papa's will, I march with my Persian and Armenian friends. The violence starts when a radical group, showing their support of the law, arrives on motorcycles, bearing bats and knives, chanting threats against women without *hijab*.

"Death on women without *hijab*! Death on women without *hijab*!"

The organized, peaceful march turns to chaos, and their scare tactics shut us down.

Defeated women, covered in *hijab*, face the new *Basiji*, a military unit Khomeini created to defend the principles of the Islamic movement. Patrolling the streets in their green or white four-by-four Blazers, they are everywhere, scoping out those who aren't following the complete *hijab*. These women receive warnings, but in some cases, are taken to *komite*, or jailed.

***

Today, my best friend, Shady, and I go out to buy some Armenian coffee. Her name translates to "happiness" in Farsi, a true description of her soul.

She breaks the news. "You know how Javad and I are madly in love?"

"Yes, I know! Tell me! You're killing me!"

"Well, he wants to marry me."

"Oh my God! I'm so happy for you, Shady!"

"Thanks, but I don't know if my parents will agree."

As we continue walking to the coffee shop, in the heat of our conversation, a *Zeinab* (female street police), who works with *Basiji*, approaches me. Apparently, according to her, my short bangs have fallen out of my *hijab*.

She rudely says, "Ma'am, cover yourself."

"What are you talking about?"

A bit louder, she demands, "Cover your hair."

"I am a Christian, and this is the best I can do."

"Don't you know that lying is a great sin?"

"Of course, but I'm not lying."

Because I speak flawless Farsi without any accent, she doesn't believe me.

"Let me see your ID!" she demands.

I pull out my ID card and hold it close to her face. She reads my name. "Ariana Mikaelian. Well, even the Madonna wore a head cover."

By this point, I'm about to explode. Shady elbows me, telling me to shut up, then pulls my *roopush* sleeve, forcing me to leave.

Most of the walk home I spend venting. "Shady, I'm so disappointed. I feel like I've been cheated. When I decided to march against the Shah, I didn't think a new government would take away my basic right of choosing how to dress. I thought I marched and voted for freedom!"

"You, me, and millions of other people, even my parents, who you know are very religious, don't think all these restrictions are fair."

"You know what, Shady? It really doesn't matter. They can put a cover on my hair, but they can't cover my mind."

A Ravaged City

DAY AFTER DAY, THE BOMBING is ceaseless. Fear is epidemic and citizens are insecure. In the mornings, most people bide their time by standing in lines to buy bread, rice, eggs, milk, and kerosene oil. In the evenings, if weather permits, many leave their homes seeking shelter at the public parks—in case of a bombing, there are no buildings to collapse on them. Some who have residences on the outskirts of town move away, like my uncles Serge and Ted and their families, who have moved to a villa. They host a lot of friends and families, even my family sometimes. Being there with my aunts and cousins is fun. But at the end of the day, I'm worried, not knowing if my house will still be standing once we return.

The ravaged city of Tehran is busy with incessant ambulances carrying injured troops or their remains. Vans with blaring megaphones ask people to donate medical supplies and blood for wounded troops, since the hospitals are in dire need. In times like these, Mom and I rush to give whatever we can. It's definitely not a time to hold back. After all, the troops are someone's son, husband, father, brother . . .

As I worry for our situation, I feel so lonely. Eda told us last night that by the end of the month, they will be leaving for Paris, then on to the U.S. My days are filled with longing for my dear sister. And before I know it, Eda, Shant, sweet Ivan, and precious Maral are gone.

***

Papa comes home from his recent trip.

"Hi, Papa!"

"Hello to you, *Baless*," he says, shaking hands with me and hugging Josh. Sometimes I miss myself as the little Ariana who would jump into Papa's arms and be tossed in the air.

Mom comes in, drying her hands. "Jacob, you look very tired. Go take your shower and then we'll talk."

As Papa comes from his shower, Mom has made him tea and I bring dates with some homemade *nazook*, the delicious cookie he loves. We all sit around the table while Josh digs in Papa's bag for souvenirs.

"So, tell me, have you heard from Eda?"

"Since you left, we have no news," Mom answers monotonically.

"God willing, they are safe." He raises his hand in reverence.

"Papa, what news do you have? What's going on in other cities?" I ask.

"Don't ask, *Baless*. It is very bad. Every town is demolished, and a chain of *hejleh* has covered every step of the way. Each picture shows a young man. It breaks my heart. Thousands of *hejlehs* defeat the purpose of blackouts. What about here?" Papa runs his shirt sleeve across his face to staunch the flow of tears he cannot control.

Mom speaks up. "It's pretty bad here, too. I spend hours standing in lines, waiting to buy food supplies and kerosene oil. Bombing is rapid every night. Some hospitals were bombed a few days ago, but the news doesn't report everything."

"Papa, whatever we know is through BBC and Radio Iraq," I say, looking at the lonely clock hanging on the wall. This reminds Papa of the news, so we all go to Papa's radio.

As he messes with the antennae, a loud, continuous siren wails. Deafening explosions follow. I feel the building move, the windows rattle, so I run to Mom's bedroom. Since we have moved to the third floor of the building, I now have a better view. "Papa, Papa, come here!" I scream. Papa, Mom, and Josh rush to the room. "Look!" I point out the window to a ball of fire shooting to the sky like a giant unleashed monster.

Papa puts his rough, blistered hand to his forehead, and with great empathy says, "That is the refinery."

We stand still, stones in shock, watching the ball take over the sky.

The radio soon announces what we already know. The refinery near Tehran has successfully been destroyed.

1983–1984
A Story to Tell

UPON HEARING THE NEWS that a ceasefire has been declared—for now—Mom decides to buy a bicycle for Josh. Wonderful news on both counts!

Josh is so happy! Mom lets him ride it in the alley where other neighbors' children usually play. He rides his bike with such pride, giving me a sense of satisfaction as if it were me riding the broken red bicycle from the old house.

***

As Mom prepares dinner, I set the table. "Ariana, go to the balcony and call Josh in for dinner," she orders.

"Sure," I say, walking towards the balcony. I look around—no Josh. Worry is eating a hole in my stomach as I head back to the kitchen and begin making the cucumber salad.

"Did you call him?" Mom asks.

Hesitating, I say, "Y-yes, but I'll try again. I didn't see him." I go back to the balcony and call him by name, loudly, but still no Josh. I *know* this will trigger Mom. "Don't worry, Mom. I'm sure he'll come home soon."

"Shut up, Ariana! Where the hell is he?! I told him to be around so he could hear me when I call him home." She rushes to the balcony, shouting for Josh at the top of her lungs. As her anger escalates, the cursing begins.

Not long after, Josh comes home. Mom walks to the dining room, and I follow. Josh stands near the door, pale and scared, in his white turtleneck sweater and jeans, which don't quite reach his ankles. As Mom yells at him, his lower lip folds into a frown.

Mom keeps cursing. I don't know what to do. She proceeds to bend down, grab her thick plastic slipper, and with one shot, throws it at him. In a flash, his forehead is covered in blood. The slipper cut him just above his eyebrow. With blood running down his face, his once white shirt is now spotted red. In shock, Josh stands frozen.

Mom bends down to pick up the other slipper. As she gets ready to aim at Josh for the second time, a fury in me takes over. I grab Mom by her shoulders and push her to the wall. "Enough, Mom! Look at him! What more do you want?" I scream. "I've got to get him to the clinic!"

As I go to get my *hijab*, Mom grabs hers, takes Josh by his hand, and charges out the door with him.

I lean back against the wall, slide down to the floor, hide my face in my headscarf, and cry. If only I had stepped in sooner, he might not have been hurt. Either way, Mom's retaliation against me is certain, but the reality of what I just did gives me pride. I protected Josh.

***

After several hours, they return home. Josh is exhausted and has eight stitches across his forehead. He can hardly make it to his bed. I manage to change his shirt and wipe his bloodied hands and body with a warm, damp towel. Josh goes to bed with a story to tell Papa, and anyone who would ask . . . of a fall from his new bicycle.

One Day at a Time

AS WE GET FURTHER into the depths of the war, missing Eda is undeniable. Every Friday, she and her sweet babies used to come and visit, filling the house with their lively innocence. Now it's filled with only their memories. As if that isn't enough, there's Ed to miss. Every day, I wait for a letter or a short phone call from my sister and brother.

Being surrounded with war and its catastrophic events, I feel so much loss. Since it began, everyone I know has either lost someone or knows of someone who has been killed. Papa's job has become even more difficult and dangerous. Papa let us know it has become mandatory for him to deliver supplies to the military base occasionally, which only intensifies my worry.

"What exactly will you be delivering, Papa?"

"I don't know yet, *Baless*. Whatever they need." He tries to brush it off by saying, "I'll be fine. Actually, the military base is protected by anti–air strike missiles, so it's safer."

"Of course, Papa." I cast my eyes down and turn away. But the unspoken truth is that he knows I don't believe a word he says.

***

Soon after Papa's announcement, he leaves to deliver supplies for the military. Weeks pass without a phone call from him. The only news we have is from my Uncle Miktar, who told Mom, "Jacob's truck was seen by his coworker heading to Abadan, near the border of Iraq, now used as a military base."

Mom and I don't want to worry Josh, so we don't talk much about Papa. We just pray.

***

Finally, after three weeks, our prayers are answered! Papa comes home, thin and dirty, but his smile is the same as he hugs Josh and shakes my hand. Papa has never embraced or kissed Mom, Eda, or me, but his handshake means a lot.

"Are you well, Jacob?" Mom asks.

Papa replies a bit too fast, a bit too loud, "Of course, I am."

"Papa, how was your trip?" I ask him, wanting to know what is happening beyond us.

"It was rough. Let me take a shower. I am filthy. There were no showers available to us."

Right then, I notice Papa, until now, had held his left hand down, hiding it from us.

"Papa, why is your finger all wrapped up?"

Papa pauses a second. "Oh, *Shoonig*. You don't miss a thing!"

"No, Papa. What happened?"

Mom takes his hand and notices the dressing on his ring finger. "What happened, Jacob?"

"It's okay," he says, pulling away. "Let me take a shower."

Mom and I set the table and prepare Papa's favorite rice dish, *garmeer pilaf*. When he finishes eating, he calls me to change the dressing on his finger. I get the medical supplies we have left over to help my papa.

"*Baless*, it's a little cut, but different than others."

I slowly begin to cut the sides of the old bandage around his finger, preparing myself for what I am about to see. As I undo the bandage, I stop for a second, gasping at a still-open wound. A section of Papa's ring finger is actually missing! "Oh, Papa!"

Mom and Josh come quickly to see.

"It's fine. It's just a little injury."

I try to hide my alarm and start applying a prescribed medicine Papa says was given to him by the military doctor. "Papa, please tell me what happened."

"As I was helping soldiers empty ammunition out of my truck, I heard an explosion, then a fiery object zoomed past by me. That's when shrapnel hit my finger. I looked down to find the tip of my finger was missing." Papa chuckles nervously to himself.

Josh, Mom, and I are shocked.

"I'm just missing the tip of my finger. Do you have any idea how many young innocent lives are missing?"

For the rest of the night, I find myself thinking of Papa's story and imagining the troops and the dangers they face every single day.

***

The bombing is incessant now, with enemy fighter jets even appearing in the daylight with their merciless raids on the neighborhoods, schools, and anywhere else they can hit. One of the most recent attacks was about ten kilometers away from my house, but the deafening sound of the explosion seemed like it was just next door.

Later that night, Mom, Josh, Papa, and I impatiently watch the news. To our surprise, the destruction is broadcast. The picture on TV shows a massive, deep hole in the ground along with many destroyed buildings and parked cars. The enormity of the destruction is unbelievable. There is no mention of lives lost, but it is reported that a government building was the missed target.

"Our area isn't safe anymore, is it, Papa?"

"I guess I underestimated Iraqi's military power. You're right, *Baless*. I don't think there is any safe place left." Papa sighs.

I wonder if the enemy's hometowns have been untouched.

With sadness in his voice, he states in a monotone, "War is a nasty game."

***

Another ceasefire has been announced. It's time for all to regroup, time for the bodies of soldiers to rest in peace. Side by side, many Armenians, along with Muslim troops, put their lives on the line to protect the country. These martyrs decorate the *hejlehs* with their names and pictures.

Since the news doesn't exactly announce how long the ceasefire will last, we have all learned to live one day at a time . . . so we do.

Najes

WITH THE ARRIVAL OF SUMMER also comes the news I'm able to take classes to prepare myself for the university's entry exam! Now that the universities are open again, I'm so excited! Hopefully, I'll be able to attend since it's something I've always dreamed of. When I ask Mom and Papa if I can take these classes, Papa, of course, has no objection. Mom doesn't disagree, but she does warn me of the expense.

I sign up, eager to start. It doesn't take long for me to realize how drastically the textbooks have changed. The history I learned in my four years of high school is no more. It's been replaced by new material without western influence. I have to study four years of revised high school textbooks just to take a college entrance exam! This is impossible! How can I learn all this material in just three months? But I am determined, so I work hard, really hard.

I attend classes with many Persian students. From a distance, we all look the same in our dark-colored *hijabs*. Some of the more religious girls are covered with *chador*. It doesn't surprise me to find out that in this institute I am the only Armenian, but I really don't feel singled out. After all, I've always been the minority, and my best friends are Persian.

I keep attending these prep classes for three months, eight hours a day, six days a week. Besides physics, literature, and math, I also have to study religion since I'm the only non-Muslim student. The teacher is a fanatical Muslim man named Ali Reza, who wears a full, ungroomed beard, shirt buttoned all the way to his throat, long sleeves, and long pants.

As soon as he reads through his attendance form, he repeats my name loudly several times. I raise my hand to let him know the name belongs to me. He stares at me with a smirk on his face and says, "Armeni, huh?"

I'm still quiet.

"You *know* you have to take these classes in order to pass the exam."

"I'm not familiar with the rules," I reply.

"Every Muslim must know the Quran. This is an Islamic country now, and everyone should proudly adhere to Islam." He doesn't even try to hide his contempt for me. "If you aren't Muslim, you have no choice. You'd better learn quickly or leave this class."

Again, I stay quiet and try my hardest not to show any emotion. I just know how badly I want to pass the exam.

Day after day, I attend my classes, including religion. A couple of the girls who are from religious Muslim families are now friends of mine, and even they don't like the way Mr. Ali Reza treats me.

***

Today, as I sit in religion class, Mr. Ali Reza walks into the room and starts talking about uncleanliness, or *najes*, from the Islamic viewpoint. *Najes* is a very strong, discriminatory word. In Islam, animals such as dogs and cats, along with animal and human waste, are considered *najes*. He speaks loudly, "Quran has said any religion but Islam is *najes*." He proceeds to rudely stare at me and repeats, "Non-Islamics are *najes!*"

I stare right back, humiliated, about to explode. My Persian Muslim friend Fatima squeezes my thigh under the table.

Mr. Ali Reza twists the knife by saying, "If you kill a mosquito on your hand and the blood comes out, that blood is also *najes!*"

Oh boy! That does it! I ignore Fatima's urgency and bravely stand up, saying, "So, Mr. Ali Reza, are you saying that if you are dying and my blood could save you, you would reject it because I am '*najes*'?"

His face turns bright red and his eyes just about pop out of his head. This time, Fatima tells me to shut up with a kick to my foot. I take a seat as class is dismissed.

Hurt and disappointed, I walk home with Fatima. Trying to comfort me, she says, "Don't worry. He's stupid. Not everyone thinks the way he does."

"Fatima, I know. I was born here. My parents and my grandparents were, too. The last time I remember someone calling me *najes* was when I was five years old and I touched the grapes in a grocery store. The grocery stocker, who was an illiterate boy, called me *najes* and threw away the grapes I'd touched, telling Mom he couldn't sell them. The owner of the grocery store ended up kicking him out and called him an ignorant idiot. Ever since that happened, I haven't heard of any of my Armenian friends or family being discriminated against like this."

Out of compassion, Fatima puts her hand on my shoulder and says, "I'm sorry, Ariana. God knows where Mr. Ali Reza comes from and what his background is. My mom says these kinds of people are new believers, who all of a sudden appear and have strong, fanatical religious beliefs."

"Thank God for people like you and your mom, Fatima."

As I try to calm myself down, I promise to get back at Mr. Ali Reza.

From that day on, till the end of the term, I deliberately touch every inch of Mr. Ali Reza's desk, chair, blackboard, and every single stick of chalk . . . and I make sure he sees me doing it.

Exam Day

I DON'T KNOW HOW prepared I am for the exam, but I go ahead and fill out the application for the test. There are many questions that don't apply to me, such as: "Have you lost immediate family in war?" "Has either your father or brother been killed in war?" "Have you lost your house due to war?" and "Have you been injured in war?" I answer "no" to all, making me feel less confident in my acceptance.

I decide to go and ask Fatima for help. On my way to her house, I pass by the college prep institute, where I accidentally see the director, Mr. Husseini.

"Oh, hello, Miss Mikaelian," he says.

"Hello, Mr. Husseini."

"Miss Mikaelian, I'm glad to see you. I want to make sure you have your book for the religion exam."

"Mr. Husseini, I'm not sure I follow. What book are you talking about?"

Looking even more surprised than me, he replies, "Didn't your religion teacher, Mr. Ali Reza, tell you that you don't have to take the Islamic portion of the exam?"

"No, Mr. Husseini. He actually told me I would have to learn the Quran to pass the religion section."

"I am so sorry, Miss Mikaelian. He should have told you. You still have time. There is a Farsi-written version of the Bible you need to study."

"I am familiar with that book, Mr. Husseini, but I will review it."

I thank Mr. Husseini and continue on my way, furiously disappointed, thinking how ignorant Ali Reza is and how desperately he wanted to hurt me.

Fatima opens the door and invites me in. Her mom is standing in the room praying quietly. We head to Fatima's room, where she helps me fill out the application.

"You know, Ariana, even if we pass the written exam, there are two other parts. One is an interview—a religious official will ask us questions to see how much we know about Islam and how often we participate in religious events—and the next part includes someone being sent to the neighborhood with our picture to ask around about our backgrounds and reputation."

"Fatima, why am I even trying?"

"Don't be disappointed, Ariana." Fatima touches my hand. "I myself don't think I'll pass, but we shall try our best together."

"I will do my best."

***

Early on the morning of the exam, Fatima and I step off the bus in the very place I used to march against the Shah. My anxiety escalates not only for myself but for the hundreds of students testing today as we hurriedly search on campus for the location of our exam.

Finally, Fatima and I find our assigned testing room. Thankfully, we are both in the same room. I open the testing packet and flip through the pages. Every question looks like gibberish to me. It seems like there isn't a single question I can answer. I decide to play the guessing game.

***

After three weeks, I hear the exam results are posted, so I buy the *Kayhan Daily Newspaper* to check for my name. My eyes scroll up and down. Nope. Turns out, I bought the newspaper just to find out "Ariana Mikaelian" is absent, although I do recognize a few Armenian names. I fold the paper, tuck it away, and decide I'm done. No university for me. No future. No getting away from Mom. I don't know how much longer I can go on with Mom's abuse and my never-ending humiliation. I am tired of feeling unsafe in my own home. It is my battlefield, but this war in my life has no chance of a ceasefire.

I pick up one of my books, sit on the balcony, and try to read. Every page is a blur. The hopeless cemetery of my heart is where I bury another one of my failures.

Perspective

AS I LIE IN MY BED, a sparkling blanket of stars stare back at me through my window. I wonder if they can see how much I miss Eda and Ed, and if they are missing me, too. The tears begin to well in my eyes when I notice a moving star. A moving star? I jump off my bed and yell, "A plane, Mom!" Then there's an explosion!

Mom rushes to wake up Josh, who's in a deep, innocent sleep. I rush to get the bag. As the siren alerts the neighborhood, we all rush down to shelter beneath the stairs. War breaks out again.

Of course, the moving star was a fighter jet, an Intruder. They fly so high all you can see is one tiny moving light. The neighbors join us, incessantly praying to be kept safe. I'm nervous and just want this roller coaster to be over. Tonight, it seems as soon as one siren alerts us of safety, another one goes off punctuating yet another attack. After the third time, Mom, Josh, and I stay in the house and don't seek shelter.

I stand near the window and look at the sky. It's funny how our perspectives change. Before the war, I would get lost searching for comfort in the stars. Now I'm searching for fighter jets.

Finally, daylight breaks. Another sleepless night is over. As I get Josh ready for school, Mom queues to buy kerosene oil. Winter is fast approaching.

Once Josh leaves, I join Mom to carry the five-gallon barrel of kerosene home. Even though the cold autumn breeze chills me to the bone, I hardly notice as my focus is on getting the barrel home—a twenty-minute walk—and up three flights of stairs.

"Ariana! Ariana!" I turn to find it's Shady calling me.

"Good morning, girl!" I put the kerosene down and hug her. "So good to see you, Shady! What are you doing here?"

"I'm helping my mom get bread. She's standing in line. Ariana, I have good news."

"What? Are you getting married?"

"No, no. We are soon moving to your alley! We'll be neighbors!"

"Oh my God! Which house?"

"Right across from yours. You'll be able to see me from your balcony."

"Really? I didn't know that house was for sale."

"It isn't. My dad knows the owner, and that's how we found out."

"So, when are you moving in?"

"Soon. Actually, in a few days."

"Oh, Shady! I can't wait for you to move in, if the bombs don't kill us first." We both grin, hug each other, and say goodbye.

Over the next few days, Shady moves into the house across the street. Now I have a friend really close by! We can see each other from our balconies and with our body language, talk to one another. We can also take shelter together and meet up in the alley afterward to talk.

***

Bombs continue to drop from the sky. Radio Iraq announces and warns the civilians in other parts of the city and surrounding towns to evacuate the targeted areas since it is "not our intention to harm civilians." Within the given time period, the citizens from these areas leave their homes in panic. The streets are flooded with people trying to find a safer place to stay (if there even is such a thing).

Most of the time, the announced areas are not bombed, but others are. It's a nerve-wracking war game. Every morning when I wake up, I thank God for letting me make it one more day.

***

Soon, Papa comes home with more devastating news. "Driving through the different towns, I've seen such havoc and decimation. Ambulances scream to overcrowded hospitals. Truckloads of deceased military troops scatter the streets. It's a scene that makes you hate your life." Papa hangs his head, shaking it slowly from side to side.

Because I have become desensitized, I don't react as I should.

After a long conversation, and as the sun goes down, a small candle is lit. Papa tunes the radio to the BBC. "The war in Iran . . ." As the news reports, an explosion rocks strong enough to make us run down and under the stairs. My family is the only one left in the building since all the neighbors have left Tehran to go north where there is less bombing.

"Jacob, when is this war going to end?" Mom cries out hysterically.

"I don't know, Liz. I really wish I had an answer."

"Papa, it seems to be getting worse after each ceasefire," I comment.

The anti–air rocket blasts fill the gap in our conversation between the bombings. Josh, hunkered down on the floor, covers his ears with his hands. Papa holds him close.

"It's okay, *Baless*. Don't be afraid. Here under the stairs, we are safe." He shakes his head in frustration. I can see the concern in Papa's face against Josh's pale skin. Mom holds the bag to her chest, cursing the situation, and I hold a small flashlight, waiting for another explosion.

This is how night turns to morning.

***

Papa leaves on another trip today, and I'm worried. Of course, I want to see him before he leaves, so I wake before the sun comes up. Fog on the kitchen window tells me the air outside is chilly as I turn the kettle on to make tea for him.

"Good morning, *Shoonig*," Papa says to me as he walks into the kitchen.

"Good morning, Papa. I made you tea. Shall I get you some?"

"Of course, *Baless*." He pulls out his chair. "Why are you up so early?"

"I couldn't sleep, Papa."

"It's a tough time. I wish you didn't have to experience this situation."

"I know, Papa, but there isn't anything anyone can do."

Mom joins us and we all enjoy a cup of black tea with some cheese sandwiches.

"Well, it's time for me to leave," Papa says, getting up and putting on his shoes and overcoat. He pats down his pocket to listen for the jingle of his keys, then shakes hands with Mom and me.

"Jacob, be careful," Mom says, looking him in the eye.

"I will be fine. You take care of yourselves."

Mom goes back to bed and I go to the balcony to watch my sweet papa walk away. With big, strong steps, he disappears into the alley. I follow his shadow as the sun tries to find its way out.

Papa's Cough

THIS MORNING, THE LOCAL NEWS announces more than twenty young children have all died in an explosion as they were celebrating a birthday party. Many others are still trapped under the rubble. Still more towns are destroyed. The news relentlessly reports such sad stories.

I need some fresh air, so I ask Mom if I can go buy some new crossword puzzle books.

"Yes, go before it's dark. On your way, get some more candlesticks and batteries."

"Will do, Mom." I wear my *rapoosh* and *hijab* and walk through the alley to a nearby street. I pass the *hejlehs* and notice a familiar picture on one. In disbelief, I pause in front of it.

The sign reads: VERAJ ABKARIAN, AGE 21. MARTYR AWARD. ARMENIAN BROTHER JOINED GOD IN ETERNITY.

Oh my God! It can't be! I rush to get the candles and the batteries, forgetting all else, and hurry home, bawling.

"What is it, Ariana?" Mom asks, concerned, as I storm into the house.

"Oh, Mom! I just saw Mrs. Sofia's son's picture on the *hejleh*."

"Oh my God! Oh, no!" She clasps her hands to her chest and falls into a chair, and we both weep bitterly.

Josh approaches me, puts his hand on my shoulder, and hesitantly asks, "Is he my school friend's big brother? Is he Hijk's brother? Is Hijk's brother dead?"

"Yes, Josh, yes." I hug my poor Josh and stroke his head. *Do you even know what happiness feels like?*

***

Rumors crop up of chemical bombs, along with a different kind of siren, which no one really takes seriously. I decide to ask Auntie Lydia about it today when she comes by for coffee.

We talk about the rumors, our doubts, and finally, we just make silly comments, until she leaves before dark.

Josh, Mom, and I, still after three weeks, wait for Papa to come home.

***

The telephone rings. I rush to answer it.

"Hello?"

"*Baless?*"

"Papa! How are you?"

"I am well, *Baless*. How are you all?" he asks between coughs.

"We're fine, Papa. When are you coming home?"

"I'll be home tomorrow. I'm close to town, but it's dark, so I have to stop for the night."

"All right, Papa. Are you sick? You're coughing so much."

"No, I'm good. I'll see you tomorrow. Say hello to your mom and Josh."

"Okay, Papa. Please hurry home."

I hang up the phone and cheer, "Papa will be home tomorrow, Mom!"

Josh grins from ear to ear and Mom praises the Lord.

***

Early the next morning, Mom and I begin preparing Papa's favorite food, *gharmir pilaf* and *abaour*.

Around noon, he arrives. Josh and I run to him with hugs and handshakes. Mom stays back.

"Thank . . . God . . . I . . . am . . . home," Papa says, coughing between each word as he talks.

"What's wrong, Jacob?" Mom asks, deep concern etched in her brows.

"Nothing. I've been coughing a little. Maybe a hot shower and hot tea will clear my chest," Papa says, heading to the bathroom.

Mom makes a cup of hot tea with ginger powder in it, a remedy for coughing. After his shower, Papa joins us. In between sips of tea, his coughing is relentless.

"Would you like to eat lunch now?" Mom seems desperate to do something to help him.

"Yes . . . I'm . . . starving," Papa replies, coughing incessantly.

Indulging in his yogurt soup, Papa begins to tell us things he has witnessed. "When I was at the military base, the air strikes were so intense, we were asked to cover our trucks under the barricaded area for days. There was no way of getting food or supplies. I survived on some Kit-Kat bars and . . ." Papa's forceful cough interrupts, "and dates."

"Here, drink more tea," Mom urges.

Papa sips some, then says, "I was inside a temporary building when I heard the explosion. I stepped outside to see where it hit, but there was no sign of fire or smoke. All was quiet, but there was this strange smell, a smell of horseradish and garlic. A military officer with a mask on his face ran toward me screaming, 'Get down! Get down!' and threw himself at me. He removed his mask, put it on my face, and forced me into the building. He then rushed me to the bathroom, took my mask off, and said, 'Monsieur, wash your hands and face with soap.' Clueless, I asked him what was going on. He told me mustard gas had been released. I looked at him with denial and asked how that was possible.

"The officer explained that a couple of weeks ago, the Iraqis had been using bombs containing mustard or nerve gas. When these bombs explode, they release chemicals that when inhaled, cause severe blistering to the lungs, internal organs, and skin. The nerve gas also attacks the nervous system. If severe enough, a person dies a horrible death."

"So, the horseradish smell was the mustard gas? Is that why you keep coughing, Papa?"

"Yes, I think so."

"Is it going to get better?" Mom asks.

"Yes, of course. I didn't inhale that much." He was not so convincing.

***

Colder days make life even more difficult. Because of the shortage of kerosene oil, we keep all the doors in the house shut, not only to conserve it, but to also keep our living room warm. The bedrooms are so cold! At night, to avoid sleeping in a cold bed, we each have a hot water bag wrapped in a towel under our covers. Then there's Papa's persistent cough. He has to see several different pulmonary specialists who prescribe inhalers. And the colder air, signaling winter's approach, only worsens his condition. But Papa has to work; he has no choice.

Hope

MOUNTING DEATH AND DESTRUCTION are proof the bombings have taken their toll on our country. With yet another ceasefire, doubled with the coming of *Norooz*, the first day of spring and the Iranian New Year, hope rekindles in the country.

Neighbors begin spring cleaning, shopping, and cooking for *Norooz*. Persian tradition includes setting their tables with *Sofreh Haft Seen*, a spread that must have seven symbolic items in Farsi beginning with the letter "s," specifically the letter "*seen*." The main items are *somagh* (sumac) for the color of the sunrise, *serkeh* (vinegar) for age and patience, *senjed* (dried fruit from the lotus tree) for love, *samanoo* (sweet pudding) for affluence, *sabzeh* (sprout) for rebirth, *sib* (apple) for health and beauty, and *sir* (garlic) for medicine. *Sekkeh* (coin) for wealth and prosperity, and *sonbol* (hyacinth), symbolizing a spring flower, are also commonly seen on the *sofreh*.

And, of course, to top off the celebration, there is always the traditional meal of *Sabzi Polo Mahi*, a rice and herb dish served with fish along with fresh-baked pastries. The divine smells tour every neighborhood.

The day is busy, and soon everyone is inside their homes listening to their radios or TVs, awaiting the announcement of the new year. Josh, Mom, and I simply watch TV and have an ordinary meal. It's almost time to celebrate when a sudden, deafening explosion rocks the house. Mom and I run to the balcony, leaving Josh, who covers his ears and shelters under the dining table. The rapid siren blares. Disappointed and angry neighbors rush to the streets, cursing at the Iraqis. In a split second, celebration turns to devastation.

The next few days bring news of more military casualties, but purposely omit lost civilian lives. Not much information is given, but every once in a while, the newspapers and TV have a picture or two of destroyed streets or buildings. Although my family and I are safe, I often worry about the people directly affected by this destruction. How do they find food and shelter? Where do they take a shower? And I can't figure out the purpose behind the ceasefires. Are they to recoup and gather more ammunition to bomb again? Or is it to return and kill, adding to the collection of innocent lives?

***

Since the schools are out for *Norooz,* and bombing is intense, once again, most people leave town. Uncle Ted offered to take us away with him to his vacation house on the outskirts of town, where it is more secure. But since his car only has room for two, I volunteer to stay home. Papa and I will join Uncle Ted and his family as soon as Papa returns from his trip.

Josh and Mom leave with Uncle Ted. As for me? I'm as happy as can be. Even the bombs can't take that away. I'll be home all by myself for two days!

To celebrate, I ask Shady over. We chitchat without worrying if Mom will listen in on our conversation. We drink Armenian coffee, and I pretend to read our fortunes in the coffee cup. And of course, we simply *must* smoke our cigarettes.

Despite the living hell outside, Shady and I giggle over her hopes to marry her Navy Seal lover. In our dream land, we celebrate Shady's wedding. When it becomes dark outside, we turn the lights out and close the doors, so the dim light of the candle won't escape.

When Shady leaves and I'm all alone, I make plans for tomorrow. I think I'll go and buy some new puzzle books, pastries, and snacks to take to Uncle Ted's when Papa comes home. It's a quiet night. No fighter jets, at least not yet. I enjoy the calm and silence in the house by reading my book, *If the Sun Dies*, by Oriana Falacci. This is how I fall asleep.

***

Waking up late to a gray sky, I make some coffee and relax on the balcony. Soon, I'm ready to head out shopping. I walk past my old school where my group used to gather, preparing to march against the Shah. I pass by *hejlehs* with familiar faces of the neighborhood kids, recalling the day I learned of Gregory's death.

I find myself on famous Nadery Street, where I can get my shopping done. I buy several puzzle books, then head to the bakery and on to the specialty store for fresh-roasted almonds and pistachios. I pass by the once-popular, five-star Nadery Hotel, which was one time filled with international tourists but now hosts injured veterans; many of whom were severely affected and injured in recent chemical bombings.

I notice some of them strolling around; some on crutches, some in wheelchairs. I tell myself perhaps they are having a better day today. Something catches my attention! As much as I try not to look, the more I get drawn to the scene. I can't take my eyes away. I see a torso of a man in a wheelchair with one arm missing from the elbow, another missing from the shoulder, and both legs missing from the knee. The man behind him, pushing his wheelchair, has burn marks on his face and a white bandage covering half of his head and one eye.

Numbly, I make my way home. Images of the injured men are forever embedded in my brain.

Once I get home, I try to organize my shopping, but I just can't. Instead, I decide to put my bed on the balcony, make myself a cup of coffee, and slip into my pajamas. I am worn-out, exhausted, so I grab my book and light a cigarette. As I exhale, the smoke swirls about my head, dissipating in the warm breeze . . . to a continuous siren.

I think. I think of my bitter childhood memories, of Matthew, the curfew, the revolution, of Uncle Andy and Ed, the death of Gregory, and, of course, how dearly I miss Eda. Then there is the war, Papa's persistent cough, and Mom's endless anger. Most of all, I think of the fear in Josh's face that never, ever goes away.

I puff on my cigarette and play with a page in my book. Folded between two pages, I find an old letter from Eda. The words I need more than anything stare right back at me. *"Stay strong. I will get you out of there."* I read it again.

Raindrops tickle my feet. I look up to the sky. The only hope that keeps me going is in Eda's letter. She has never broken a promise.

The sky rumbles and the rain pours. I scoot my belongings to the kitchen floor, leaving the door open, and watch and listen with fascination to the rain. There's something about how the sky gets dark and the lightning can be seen before the thunder sounds. Then it pours, and the air smells fresh and clean. Every darkness is washed away.

Calmness spreads, as if nothing ever happened. It's a new beginning. And it's with that hope I hold onto Eda's promise. I close my eyes and pray, pray for the day I can begin my life.

Epilogue

IT'S BEEN FIVE YEARS since I graduated from high school. With Ed and Eda gone, I have become Mom's punching bag. I protect Josh, who is still in school, as much as I can. And Papa, despite his respiratory ailment from the mustard gas, still works hard and never complains. His feelings, whether physical or emotional, always translate into a smile.

The war continues, with the surrounding cities and southern provinces mostly destroyed and only a few places in the capital demolished. Most of the time, when we are in the shelter and our house is rattling, we can still hear the air strikes or bombs that have been dropped hundreds of kilometers away. I can't imagine what the sound would be like if it happened over my house!

Then there's the news, which hardly announces the hit targets; like the Mehrabad Airport and a few residential buildings. Still, reports of military casualties are rarely publicized. Gasoline and food continue to be in short supply, but in the black market, even Western and European supplies are available. Money can buy anything; after all, money would soon grant me a visa!

After years of battling with Mom's unexplained rage and her extreme narcissism, both of which nearly destroyed my life, I was at the edge of a nervous breakdown. It was Eda who kept giving me hope. She would call every chance she had, trying to convince Mom to let me leave Iran. Of course, after every conversation, Mom's anger would escalate, blaming me for complaining to Eda.

I did finally apply for a passport, thanks to Eda's encouragement. When I got it, in order to keep it safe from Mom, I had to carry it on me wherever I went. Finally, one day, when I found myself alone with Papa, with tears in my eyes, I said, "Papa, I cannot take this anymore. I can't breathe in this house. Please help me get out of here."

In his kind voice, he replied, *"Baless,* you've got your wings. You need to fly. I'm not going to keep you caged. I haven't wanted you to leave because I didn't want you to face difficulties on your own, but I see dealing with your mother is worse. I will convince her you need to leave."

"Really, Papa? I can't believe this! Thank you!"

Papa gave me his signature smile.

The next obstacle was to acquire a visa. Since most embassies were shut down due to the war, the last one still operating was that of Greece, in Tehran. Somehow, Papa was able to get me one through bribery. Yes, cash and a couple of bottles of Johnnie Walker Black Label work wonders!

In October of 1985, I left my papa and little Josh, who refused to go to the airport with me. He just hid under his blanket and said, "You're leaving me behind. Go away." His words broke my heart, but I had no choice. Escaping from Mom's Hell on Earth was the only way I would survive.

Soon after arriving in Athens, Greece, I learned from a phone conversation with Josh that an Iraqi bomb had demolished the hospital in our Tehran neighborhood. The tremors from this attack caused windows to shatter and walls to crack in the surrounding houses, and this sadly included ours. A part of me wanted to be with Josh and Papa, but then again, there was no turning back now. I proceeded to apply for a U.S. refugee program, the only way for me to reach America. To support myself in the meantime, I worked as a housekeeper, child caretaker, and dishwasher. And every now and then, Eda would send me money and clothing.

On April 7, 1987, after nearly two years, I arrived in the United States, the "Land of the Free." I successfully earned my cosmetology license, along with an associate degree of science in natural health. In 1990, I married an ambitious, selfless, loving man, and in 1995, we became official U.S. citizens. Together, we have two grown children: a son, Armo, and a daughter, Tee—both of whom I am immensely proud.

The rest of my family has since joined Eda and me in America. Ed has six children and nine grandchildren and works in the construction industry. My sweet Eda lost Shant to cancer but remarried a kind, compassionate man. She also lost her loving son, Ivan, in a tragic accident. He left behind a widow and two beautiful boys. Eda's lovely daughter, Maral, is married to a gentle man who has two children. Together, they have a new baby girl. And little Josh has pursued a career in technology and enjoys photography and gardening.

Mom, in her old age, despite being diagnosed with dementia, has maintained her narcissistic behaviors. She lives just one mile away from me and depends on my siblings and me to care for and support her. As Jesus asked us to do, I have forgiven her heartless abuse, but I can never forget.

Finally, my beloved papa, after many years of suffering with COPD, lost his battle, just ten months after his only remaining sibling, Uncle Miktar, passed away. Looking back, I believe Papa was aware of Mom's vicious behavior all along. But since he couldn't solve the issues, and he didn't want the family to be disgraced, he chose not to face it, hoping the best for us.

***

Once again, I sift through a box of pictures, and there are some new ones. I lay them down on the floor, as I sit near the window of my room. There is Papa, cousin Nina, little Josh, and me at the beach. Another one of Eda and me at her wedding. There is a group picture of Eda's sixtieth birthday with the loving faces of Papa and Ivan, who have faded away but left us with many cherished memories I hold this picture to my heart as a tidal wave of emotions flow over me. For a moment, I drift away.

Every joy from my childhood ended in despair, leaving an ongoing battle within the deepest cavern of my soul. Yet today, surrounded by loving people and God's grace, I have found the strength and hope to move forward. My battles will never subdue nor defeat me.